Prekindergarten Learning & Development Guidelines

Developed for the

Child Development Division
California Department of Education

by the

Health and Education Communication Consultants
Berkeley, California

Publishing Information

The *Prekindergarten Learning and Development Guidelines* was funded by the Child Development Division, California Department of Education, and developed by Health and Education Communication Consultants. It was edited by Janet Lundin, working in cooperation with Sharon Hawley, Consultant, Child Development Divison. Dixie Abbott, Gloria Barreiro, and Faye Ong assisted with the editing. It was designed and prepared for printing by the staff of CDE Press, with the cover and interior design created and prepared by Juan Sanchez. Typesetting was done by Jeannette Huff, Gloria Barreiro, and Jamie Contreras. It was published by the Department, 1430 N Street, Sacramento, California (mailing address: P.O. Box 944272, Sacramento, CA 94244-2720). It was distributed under the provisions of the Library Distribution Act and *Government Code* Section 11096.

ISBN 0-8011-1514-0

Photo Credits

The photographs in this publication were provided by John Jernegan and Linda Broach.

Ordering Information

Copies of this publication are available for $13.50 each, plus shipping and handling charges. California residents are charged sales tax. Orders may be sent to the California Department of Education, CDE Press, Sales Office, P.O. Box 271, Sacramento, CA 95812-0271; FAX (916) 323-0823. See page 192 for complete information on payment, including credit card purchases. Prices on all publications are subject to change.

A partial list of other educational resources available from the Department appears on page 192. In addition, an illustrated catalog describing publications, videos, and other instructional media available from the Department can be obtained without charge by writing to the address given above or by calling the Sales Office at (916) 445-1260.

Notice

The guidance in *Prekindergarten Learning and Development Guidelines* is not binding on local educational agencies or other entities. Except for the statutes, regulations, and court decisions that are referenced herein, the document is exemplary, and compliance with it is not mandatory. (See *Education Code* Section 33308.5.)

Prepared for publication
by CSEA members.

Contents

Foreword

California's Commitment to Young Children

PROVIDING A HIGH-QUALITY EDUCATION FOR STUDENTS IS A KEY TO THIS NATION'S FUTURE well-being, and in California the call for better educational opportunities for *all* children—including preschoolers—has been loud and clear. We know now that what happens early in a child's life is incredibly important to that child's future success.

In fact, research on the development of the brain indicates that by the time children reach age three, their brains are twice as active as those of adults. Equally important are the ages of three through five, when children continue to acquire and practice new skills and to discover the joy of learning. Because many educators now agree that organized educational efforts should begin in preschool, the question becomes—what kind of education is appropriate for this age group?

This document, *Prekindergarten Learning and Development Guidelines,* was developed to address that fundamental question. To find the answers, I convened a panel of nationally recognized experts and also asked that successful preschool educators from across the country be interviewed for this document.

Everyone agreed that all children are natural learners and that the challenge to preschool educators is to provide appropriate environments that will expand children's learning and social skills. Young children are energetic learners, and the guidelines call for high-quality preschool programs that work closely with family members and nurture children's learning in appropriate ways. This resource presents a vision of adults throughout our communities helping to enrich young children's appreciation of themselves, of others, of learning, and of life.

These guidelines also build toward our goal of offering universal preschool to all three- and four-year-olds in California. Universal preschool provides an equal opportunity for all children to have access to programs that prepare them for primary school, and it is a win-win situation for both students and educators.

Universal preschool is the next big idea that our nation must embrace. That idea is as big as and more important than putting a man on the moon. In the meantime I hope that our expanding network of early childhood educators and parents will find this document useful. I wish you success in your work to provide high-quality preschool programs.

Delaine Eastin
State Superintendent of Public Instruction

Acknowledgments

T HE CREATION OF THIS GUIDE INVOLVED MANY PEOPLE. THEY INCLUDED (1) A NATIONAL panel of experts in early childhood development and preschool programming; (2) a writing and development team from Health and Education Communication Consultants in Berkeley, California; (3) staff from the California Department of Education/Child Development Division (CDE/CDD); (4) preschool teachers and program directors across the country at sites that were visited as a part of the research for the project; and (5) focus group participants representing the various audiences of the guide.

Expert Panel

Collectively, members of the Expert Panel represent both academic and practical perspectives in all of the aspects addressed in the *Prekindergarten Learning and Development Guidelines*. The guidelines and rationales in this guide were generated by the Expert Panel during three meetings held in Berkeley, California, from November 1998 through April 1999. Each panel member and his or her area or areas of expertise are listed below:

Donald Bailey, *Director*
Frank Porter Graham Child Development Center
University of North Carolina, Chapel Hill
Chapel Hill, North Carolina
(Early childhood special education and early intervention and family support)

Goldie Bemel, *Director*
Child Development Programs
Burbank Unified School District
Burbank, California
(Child development and preservice education)

Linda Espinosa
College of Education
University of Missouri
Columbia, Missouri
(Early childhood curriculum, second-language acquisition, and parent involvement)

Paul Giganti, *Director*
Bay Area Mathematics Project
University of California, Berkeley
Berkeley, California
(Mathematics education of young children)

Dave Gordon, *Superintendent*
Elk Grove Unified School District
Sacramento, California
(Preschool policy)

Judy Guilkey-Amado, *Director*
Elementary Education
Vallejo City Unified School District
Vallejo, California
(Preservice and in-service education and school readiness and transitions)

Susan D. Holloway
Graduate School of Education
University of California, Berkeley
Berkeley, California
(Families and early childhood educators in diverse cultures and relationships between families and educational institutions)

Yolanda Jenkins
Educational Technology Consultant
Oakland, California
(Early childhood technology)

Lilian G. Katz, *Director*
ERIC Clearinghouse on Elementary and Early Childhood Education
University of Illinois
Champaign, Illinois
(Preschool teaching and curriculum)

Alice Klein
Institute of Human Development
University of California, Berkeley
Berkeley, California
(Cognitive development and early mathematical development and education)

Adria Kline
Reading Education
California State University, San Bernardino
San Bernardino, California
(Early literacy and early intervention)

Linda Kroll
Department of Education
Mills College
Oakland, California
(Preservice and in-service education, literacy development and learning, and cognitive development)

Anne Kuschner
California Institute on Human Services
Sonoma State University
Rohnert Park, California
(Early childhood special education and in-service education)

Peter Mangione
Center for Child and Family Studies
WestEd
Sausalito, California
(Social–emotional, language, and cognitive development and learning; transitions to school)

Samuel J. Meisels
School of Education
University of Michigan, Ann Arbor
Ann Arbor, Michigan
(Screening and assessment of young children's development, policy development, and children with disabilities)

Jean Monroe
Early Childhood Education/Child Development Consultant
Oakland, California
(Cultural diversity, curriculum and program development, and staff development)

Evelyn Moore, *Executive Director*
National Black Child Development Institute
Washington, D.C.
(Policy development, social action for young children, and cultural diversity)

Robert Pianta
Curry School of Education
University of Virginia
Charlottesville, Virginia
(Social development, relationships between children and teachers, and transition to kindergarten)

Theresa Roberts
College of Education
California State University, Sacramento
Sacramento, California
(Prekindergarten through first grade literacy development in multilingual classroom settings)

Tina Ruppelt
APEX Online Learning
Seattle, Washington
(Early childhood technology)

Prentice Starkey
School of Education
University of California, Berkeley
Berkeley, California
(Early childhood education and early cognitive and mathematical development)

Marcy Whitebook
Institute of Industrial Relations
University of California, Berkeley
Berkeley, California
(Recruitment, retention, and professional development of early childhood workforce)

Patricia Wolfe
Excellence in Educational Training
Napa, California
(Growth and development of the brain in children from birth through age five)

Norman Yee, *Executive Director*
Wu Yee Children's Services
San Francisco, California
(Cultural diversity and children's services)

Marlene Zepeda
Department of Child and Family Studies
California State University, Los Angeles
Los Angeles, California
(Child development, family involvement, and cultural diversity)

Edward Zigler, *Director*
Yale Bush Center in Child Development and Social Policy
Yale University
New Haven, Connecticut
(Social policy development and research and early childhood education)

Kayla Kirsch, Christina Merkley, and **Tomi Nagai-Rothe,** from The Grove Consultants International, facilitated and graphically recorded three meetings of the Expert Panel; and **Anthony DeVenuta**, from DeVenuta and Associates, audiotaped and transcribed the meetings of the panel.

Health and Education Communication Consultants

The staff members from Health and Education Communication Consultants in Berkeley, California, are listed as follows:

Linda Broatch, *Project Director*

Lisa Hunter, *Principal Investigator*

Donna Lloyd-Kolkin, *Editorial Director*

Hank Resnik, *Lead Writer*

Jane Stern, *School Liaison Consultant*

Marilyn White, *Administrative Assistant*

California Department of Education

Staff members from the California Department of Education are listed as follows:

Leslie Fausset, *Deputy Superintendent,* Educational Policy, Curriculum, and Department Management

Kathy B. Lewis, *Deputy Superintendent,* Child, Youth and Family Services Branch

Michael Jett, *Director,* Child Development Division

Sharon Hawley, *Consultant,* Child Development Division

Maria Balakshin, *Director,* Child Development Division (retired)

Janet Poole, *Administrator,* Child Development Division (retired)

Diane Levin, *Education Policy Advisor to the Chief Deputy Superintendent for Accountability and Administration*

Jan Agee, *Assistant Director,* Communications Office

Preschools in the Project

Several preschools were visited as a part of the project's research. They were selected on the basis of recommendations from the CDE/CDD, the Expert Panel members, California's Early Childhood Mentor Programs, and the National Center to Enhance Early Development and Learning.

Bloomingdale Family Center Head Start Program
Susan Feingold, *Director*
New York, New York

Columbus Elementary School
Connie Murphy, *Preschool Teacher*
Berkeley, California

Darwin Center Head Start
Ermina Gutierrez, *Site Supervisor*
Hayward, California

Edith Storey Preschool
Ku Yang, *Head Teacher*
Fresno, California

Evergreen Community School
Alise Shafer, *Director*
Santa Monica, California

Frank Porter Graham Child Development Center
Debby Cryer, *Child Care Program Director*
University of North Carolina, Chapel Hill
Chapel Hill, North Carolina

Madison Center Head Start
Susan Kerney, *Head Teacher*
Fresno, California

School Readiness Language Development Program
Ellen Owens, *Head Teacher*
Paulette McFarland, Head Teacher
Van Nuys Elementary School
Van Nuys, California

Will Rogers State Preschool
Maria Martinez, *Head Teacher*
Santa Monica, California

Focus Groups

Seven focus groups were conducted by **Katherine Hayes**, from Juarez and Associates in Los Angeles, at Berkeley, Los Angeles, and Fresno. Participants were preschool teachers, program directors from early childhood education programs, college instructors, and parents.

PART ONE
Background

CHAPTER 1

Introduction

THE GOAL OF *PREKINDERGARTEN LEARNING AND DEVELOPMENT GUIDELINES* IS to provide the guidance needed by preschool directors and teachers to build high-quality programs that prepare children to arrive in kindergarten well-prepared for the new learning and curriculum content they will encounter there. In this way California's three- through five-year-olds will have the foundational skills needed to achieve academic success throughout their school careers and to become productive citizens.

This section describes the purpose and audience for this guide and the context of preschool education. The purpose of this section is to present an overview of key issues that should be taken into account in planning and implementing a high-quality preschool program.

The primary audience for this publication is people who are responsible for preschool program planning. When the document is used in combination with parent materials, videotapes, and teacher training materials, it can also be helpful and informative to a broader audience of policymakers, school administrators, teaching staff, parents, and others who are concerned about improving the quality of preschools.

Need for the Guidelines

This publication is a response to the need for clear guidelines about what constitutes high-quality programming across a broad spectrum of curriculum and practice for preschools. It also takes into account what high-quality preschool programming means in the context of California's move toward higher expectations for all students at the elementary and secondary school levels. It refers to and complements policies adopted by the State Board of Education and documents published by the California Department of Education.

The guidelines in these pages present a broad picture of high-quality programming that can be adjusted to meet the needs of California's diverse preschool settings and communities. Although the guidelines are not mandatory, they represent the best practices in early childhood education and are strongly recommended by the California Department of Education for all prekindergarten programs.[1]

This publication recognizes that one of the great attractions for professionals in early childhood education is its quality of creativity and discovery of how children learn. The publication does not attempt to prescribe exactly what should be happening in a program at any given time or specifically what should be taught and what methods should be used. There is, in fact, no single "correct" model of a preschool program.

Related Publications

This document is to be used in conjunction with other initiatives supported by the California Department of Education. Descriptions of these publications follow:

◆ *First Class: A Guide for Early Primary Education.* This comprehensive guide, published in 1999, offers practical, detailed, research-based information to implement an effective learning program for children from ages four through six. *First Class,* which offers a wealth of helpful information, is referred to in numerous places throughout this document as an additional resource.

◆ *Ready to Learn: Quality Preschools for California in the 21st Century.* This report, published in 1998, presents the findings and recommendations of the Universal Preschool Task Force. It offers details and proposals for a

---

[1]The guidelines in the *Prekindergarten Learning and Development Guidelines* are recommendations and are distinct from program standards. When the Desired Results Program Performance Standards are published, they will contain the requirements for funding center-based programs and family child care home networks under contract with the Child Development Division of the California Department of Education.

comprehensive program that will ensure the availability of half-day preschool programs for all three- and four-year-old children. *Ready to Learn* represents the best thinking of leaders in the field on the premise that now is the time to move ahead with a realistic and feasible plan.

◆ Content standards and curriculum frameworks for reading/language arts and mathematics that were adopted and published by the State Board of Education from 1997 through 1999. The content standards and frameworks define new and higher expectations for all of California's students in kindergarten through grade twelve. As California raises its expectations for all students, children need, more than ever before, a wide variety of experiences that will stimulate their cognitive, social, physical, and emotional growth during the preschool years.

Organization of the Content

The document is divided into three main sections. Part 1 presents the background and context of early childhood education, with a particular focus on recent developments in the field in California. Part 2 consists of guidelines for all the major areas of a high-quality preschool program. Several important themes—children with special needs, cultural diversity, parent and family involvement, assessment, and professional development—are woven throughout the document. Part 3 offers a variety of resources for program implementation and improvement.

The guidelines, examples, and brief vignettes in this document offer clear directions on the best practices for preschool professionals. This material draws on extensive research, on the collective professional experience of the expert panel that helped to develop the guidelines, and on visits to the sites of exemplary programs throughout California and in other states. The guidelines represent a solid foundation on which to build high-quality preschool programs for California's future.

CHAPTER 2

Current Issues in Early Childhood Education

T HIS CHAPTER CONSISTS OF TWO MAJOR SECTIONS. THE FIRST ELABORATES ON a variety of issues that are central to early childhood and preschool education throughout the United States. The second focuses specifically on recent developments in early childhood and preschool education in California.

General Issues

The general issues in this section cover the need for high-quality preschool programs, the impact of societal changes on the need for preschool education, the contributions of research on the development of the brain, and the preparation of young children for kindergarten.

Evidence from Research

Common sense dictates that the preschool years are critically important for children's later development and their subsequent performance in school. As detailed in *Ready to Learn* (California Department of Education 1998e), this premise has been substantiated in recent years by a wide body of research:

◆ Children in high-quality child development settings engage in more complex activities with peers and materials and score higher on standardized measures of school readiness (University of Colorado 1995; Kontos and others 1994; Whitebook, Howes, and Phillips 1990; Kisker and others 1991; Howes and Hamilton 1993).

◆ Children who attend high-quality child care programs show significant cognitive gains during early childhood and perform better academically compared with children in low-quality programs (Burchinal, Lee, and Ramey 1989; Layzer, Goodson, and Moss 1993; Campbell and Ramey 1994; National Academy Press 1990). Recent research shows that the effects of quality in preschool have an enduring impact at least through the second grade (Peisner-Feinberg and others 1999).

◆ Longitudinal studies of high-quality early childhood programs reveal that their positive effects persist well into adolescence and adulthood. A 27-year follow-up study of the Perry Preschool Program in Ypsilanti, Michigan, showed that children from low-income families who attended preschool as four-year-olds had fewer criminal arrests and higher levels of social functioning than did others. This program yielded more than $7 in benefits for every $1 invested (Berrueta-Clement and others 1984; Schweinhart and Weikart 1997; Lally, Mangione, and Honig 1988).

In addition, research (Howes and Hamilton 1993) shows that, overall, preschoolers in high-quality programs:

◆ Enter kindergarten with skills needed to be successful with school tasks.

◆ Show greater knowledge of verbal and numerical concepts.

◆ Receive higher ratings on social competence.

◆ Show greater task orientation.

◆ Are more likely to make normal progress through the primary grades.

◆ Are less often retained or placed in special education classes.

The Cost, Quality, and Outcomes Team Study (Peisner-Feinberg and others 1999), one of the most exhaustive recent national surveys of early childhood education, found that:

- High-quality child care is an important element in achieving the national goal of having all children ready for school.

- High-quality child care continues to predict positively children's performance well into their school careers.

- Children who have traditionally been at risk of not doing well in school are affected more by the quality of child care experiences than are other children.

- The quality of child care classroom practices was related to children's cognitive development, while the closeness of the relationship between the child care teacher and each child influenced children's social development through the early school years.

THE ABECEDARIAN PROJECT

One of the most noteworthy recent reports on the positive effects of high-quality early childhood education focused on the Abecedarian Project, "a carefully controlled study in which 57 infants from low-income families were randomly assigned to receive early intervention in a high-quality child care setting [through age five] and 54 were in a control group." The project's findings included:

- Both groups "were initially comparable with respect to scores on infant mental and motor tests. However, from the age of 18 months and through the completion of the child care program, children in the intervention group had significantly higher scores on mental tests than children in the control group. Follow-up cognitive assessments completed at ages 12 and 15 years showed that the intervention group continued to have higher average scores on mental tests."

- Children who received early educational intervention scored significantly higher on achievement tests of reading and math from the primary grades through middle adolescence.

- "[In] a young-adult follow-up assessment of study participants . . . young adults who received early educational intervention had significantly higher mental test scores from toddlerhood through age 21 than did [the control group.]"

- The intervention group "were significantly more likely still to be in school at age 21– 40% of the intervention group compared with 20% of the control group."

- "A significant difference was also found for the percent of young adults who [had] ever attended a four-year college. About 35% of the young adults in the intervention group had either graduated from or were at the time of the assessment attending a four-year college or university. In contrast, only about 14% in the control group had done so."

  — F. Campbell and C. Ramey, *Early Learning, Later Success: The Abecedarian Study*

Other references for this topic follow:

Alexander, K. L., and D. R. Entwisle. 1988. "Achievement in the First Two Years of School: Patterns and Processes," *Monographs of the Society for Research in Child Development,* Vol. 53 (Serial no. 218).

Lazar, I., and others. 1982. "Lasting Effects of Early Education: A Report from the Consortium for Longitudinal Studies," in *Monographs of the Society for Research in Child Development,* no. 47 (Serial no. 195). Chicago: University of Chicago Press.

The Need for High-Quality Preschool Programs

Despite growing evidence of the importance and long-term beneficial effects of early childhood education, a number of studies have shown that the quality of typical child care programs in the United States is considerably below what is considered good practice (Burchinal and others 1996; University of Colorado 1995; Layzer, Goodson, and Moss 1993). A synthesis of this research (Love, Schochet, and Meckstrom 1996) suggests that the poor to mediocre quality is so consistent as to raise broad concern about the quality of care in early childhood settings nationwide.

The Impact of Societal Changes

Largely as a result of changes in the American family in recent decades, the field of early childhood education has also changed both in California and the rest of the nation. The primary change is that far more families and children now need child care and preschool facilities than they have in the past.

Several trends in American family life have contributed to dramatic growth in the preschool population:

- First, more mothers are working outside the home. From 1992 through 2005, the labor force participation rate for women between the ages of twenty-five and fifty-four is projected to increase from 75 percent to 83 percent, leading to the further decline in the number of mothers who can provide full-time care for their children in the home (Hernandez 1995).

- Second, there are more single-parent families. Since 1950 the percentage of children living in one-parent families has nearly tripled. One in four American children now lives in a single-parent family, usually headed by a female head of household who typically receives little or no financial help from the child's father.

- In addition, more young children are living in poverty and urgently need high-quality preschool programs. Poor children are statistically more likely to suffer poor health, maltreatment, and later academic failure (Carnegie Task Force 1994).

Contributions of Research on Brain Development

Research on the development of the brain and human intelligence increasingly suggests that positive stimulation of the brain during the early years creates the foundation for a child's lifelong thinking, attitudes, and behavior.

Marian Diamond (Diamond and Hopson 1998) and a research team at the University of California, Berkeley, for example, have found that enriched environments can influence brain growth significantly. According to Diamond, an enriched environment:

- Includes a steady source of positive emotional support
- Provides a nutritious diet with enough protein, vitamins, minerals, and calories

- Stimulates all the senses (but not necessarily all at once)
- Has an atmosphere free of undue pressure and stress but suffused with a degree of pleasurable intensity
- Presents a series of novel challenges that are neither too easy nor too difficult for children at their stages of development
- Allows social interaction for a significant percentage of activities
- Promotes development of a broad range of mental, physical, aesthetic, social, and emotional skills and interests
- Gives children an opportunity to choose many of their efforts and to modify them
- Allows children to be active participants rather than passive observers

Conversely, a stressful environment and a lack of stimulation can impair healthy brain development. Early interventions should focus on providing stability, predictability, and information. A major way to affect a stressed child is to provide predictability, nurturance, support, and cognitive intervention, all of which make a child feel safe, comfortable, and loved (Lally 1997).

Table 1

RETHINKING THE BRAIN	
Old Thinking	**New Thinking**
How the brain develops depends on the genes you are born with.	How the brain develops hinges on a complex interplay between the genes you are born with and the experiences you have.
The experiences you have before the age of three have limited impact on later development.	Early experiences have a decisive impact on the architecture of the brain and on the nature and extent of adult capacities.
A secure relationship with a primary caregiver creates a favorable context for early development and learning.	Early interactions do not just create a context; they directly affect the way the brain is "wired."
Brain development is linear: The brain's capacity to learn and change grows steadily as an infant progresses toward adulthood.	Brain development is nonlinear: there are prime times for acquiring different kinds of knowledge and skills.
A toddler's brain is much less active than the brain of a college student.	By the time children reach age three, their brains are twice as active as those of adults. Activity levels drop during adolescence.

Source: Shore, R. 1997. *Rethinking the Brain: New Insights into Early Development.* New York: Families and Work Institute.

LANGUAGE DEVELOPMENT AND THE BRAIN

When a baby is born, its brain can perceive the individual sounds of all of the estimated 6,000 languages in the world. Very few children, however, are exposed to more than one, or possibly two, languages, and the sounds the child hears repeatedly will be strengthened, while the ones it doesn't hear will begin to fade away. By adolescence this remarkable ability to speak any language unaccented and with little or no formal instruction is greatly diminished or, for most of us, is lost.

Talking and reading to the young child are immeasurable gifts. These practices not only stimulate the language center of the brain; they expand vocabulary and understanding, stimulate imagination, and foster the emotional growth of the child.

— Patricia Wolfe, Expert Panel member

Preparation of Young Children for Kindergarten

The trend throughout the country toward higher standards for educational achievement in kindergarten through grade twelve has led to concern among parents and teachers that children may be unprepared for the school tasks that await them. Kindergarten teachers have estimated that each year as many as 30 percent of their entering students are not ready to learn in the classroom. In the past some experts defined *school readiness* primarily as readiness for reading. The prevailing view today, however, is that readiness reflects a range of dimensions, such as a child's health and physical development, social and emotional development, approaches to learning, language and communicative skills, and cognition and general knowledge (National Educational Goals Panel 1998; California Department of Education 1997a). To that end the National Educational Goals Panel established three objectives related to its school readiness goal:

1. All children will have access to high-quality and developmentally appropriate preschool programs that help prepare children for elementary school.

2. All parents in the United States will be their children's first teacher and devote time each day to helping their preschool children learn, and parents will have access to the training and support they need.

3. Children will receive the nutrition, physical activity, and health care needed to arrive at school with healthy minds and bodies and to maintain the mental alertness necessary to be prepared to learn, and the number of low-birthweight babies will be significantly reduced through enhanced prenatal health systems.

In many ways these goals represent an important departure from past thinking. They acknowledge that the well-being of young children is a shared responsibility between family and society and that collaboration across sectors and institutions is required. The goals also acknowledge that:

◆ All children, not just some of them, are entitled to early experiences that will foster their optimal development.

◆ Academically driven definitions of readiness that have previously been widely accepted need to be broadened to incorporate physical, social, and emotional well-being.

◆ A connection exists between children's early development and learning and their later success in school and in life (National Educational Goals Panel 1998).

Helping young children make a successful transition from home or from an early care and education setting to kindergarten has received increased attention in recent years. The development of programs and activities involving parents, early childhood educators, and elementary school staff is providing support for this important process (California Department of Education 1997a).

The California Context

A number of demographic and social trends in California have had a significant impact in recent years on the field of early childhood education. Perhaps the most important trend, according to demographic profiles developed by the California Department of Education, is that the school population is growing dramatically. Elementary school enrollments are projected to grow through 2006. (For more information see the Web site for Ed-Data <http://www.ed-data.k12.ca.us/>.)

Changes in the Welfare System

As the population of young children increases, so does the demand for child care. Major changes in the welfare system have contributed significantly to this trend. In response to federal welfare reform legislation, the state legislature created the California Work Opportunity and Responsibility to Kids (CalWORKs) program, which focuses on moving families from welfare dependency to work and, ultimately, to self-sufficiency. Participants in the CalWORKs program are required to engage in work or work preparation activities and are provided with an array of welfare-to-work services, including child care. These child care services are provided primarily in private child care settings, including child care centers, family child care homes, and in-home care. The program is administered jointly by the California Department of Social Services and the California Department of Education through alternative payment programs.

PROFILE OF PRESCHOOL CHILDREN IN CALIFORNIA

- Number of preschool-age children in California aged three, four, and five years old in 2000: 1,559,320*

- Total number of children from birth through age five estimated to be served in state and federal programs:

  California Department of Education programs: 333,949[†]

  Early Head Start: 6,504[‡]

  Head Start: 91,163[‡]

- Ethnic breakdown of children from birth to four years old (estimate for 2000)[§]

Hispanic	48%
White	34%
African American	11%
Asian/Pacific Islander	7%

- Number of limited-English-proficient children in kindergarten in 1999-00: 165,776 (36.1% of a total of 459,742)[§]

[*]Census 2000 data for California <http://www.census.gov/>.

[†]Based on California Department of Education (CDE), Management Systems data reports from FFY 1999-00, CD-800, and the CDE Survey on Statewide Participation in Subsidized Child Care, December 15, 2000 for SFY 1999-00.

[‡]Administration for Children and Families, U.S. Department of Health and Human Services, Head Start Bureau, 2002.

[§]The source for these figures may be found at the Web site for Ed-Data <http://www.ed-data.k12.ca.us/>.

YOUNG CHILDREN LIVING IN POVERTY

Over one quarter (28.6%) of young children under age five [in California] lives in poverty ($16,450 or less annual income for a family of four in 1998). This is the case even though most of their parents are working. Young children are the poorest age group among all Californians; they are more likely to be poor than older children, adults, and seniors. Yet, they are in the most vulnerable stage of development, with their environment having a substantial impact on how they grow, how well they learn, and how they interact with others. Research unequivocally shows that growing up in poverty affects children's cognitive and physical development. Moreover, living with very limited economic resources has an especially profound impact on children in their earliest years.

— Children Now, *California Report Card 1999: How Our Youngest Children Are Faring*

Universal Preschool

To improve educational results for all children in California, the State Superintendent of Public Instruction's Universal Preschool Task Force recommended that California "offer publicly funded universal preschool within ten years to all three- and four-year-old children in California for at least half the day during the regular school year" (California Department of Education 1998e). The report's six major recommendations provide guidance for full implementation of universally available preschool.

Universal preschool is an integral part of the Superintendent's agenda for improved student achievement in California. When this recommendation is implemented, California will join Georgia and New York as a national leader in prekindergarten education.

Desired Results for Children and Families

Currently being developed, the system Desired Results for Children and Families will serve as the umbrella for all of the California Department of Education/Child Development Division (CDE/CDD) child care and development initiatives. This system of standards, assessment, and accountability focuses on six desired results for children and families. Many factors contribute to the achievement of desired results, and each program contributes in unique ways. The system includes new program standards to support the achievement of desired results for children and families and procedures for implementing program standards and for evaluating the achievement of results. Tools and procedures are being designed to document the progress made by children and families in achieving desired results. This information will be used to help practitioners improve their child care and development services and to help the CDE in targeting training and technical assistance. The primary objective of Desired Results for Children and Families is to measure how well children, families, and programs are doing in meeting six broad desired results. For CDE/CDD programs a *desired result* is defined as a condition of well-being for children and families. The six desired results for children and families are as follows:

1. Children are personally and socially competent.
2. Children are effective learners.
3. Children show physical and motor competencies.
4. Children are safe and healthy.
5. Families support their children's learning and development.
6. Families achieve their goals.

(More information on this system appears in Appendix B, "Desired Results for Children and Families," and in Appendix C, "California Department of Education Initiatives.")

Development of Foundational Skills in Language, Literacy, and Mathematics

In 1997-98 the State Board of Education adopted new, more rigorous content standards and frameworks for reading/language arts and mathematics for kindergarten through grade twelve. These new standards, particularly those affecting the development of language, reading, and mathematics skills, are of great importance to preschool educators. Higher expectations in kindergarten and the primary grades will require children to enter kindergarten better prepared than ever before for new learning and skill development. (The "Program Quality Standards" section in Part 3 of this publication contains a complete listing of the content standards.)

Considerable work has been done to establish prekindergarten grade-level expectations for language arts. For example, the State Superintendent of Public Instruction, the California State Board of Education, and the California Commission on Teacher Credentialing collaborated to develop *Teaching Reading,* a program advisory on early reading instruction. This document offers examples of skill benchmarks for prekindergarten children (California Department of Education 1996b, p. 14):

◆ Recognize print in the environment.

◆ Distinguish separate words.

◆ Recognize rhyming words.

◆ Know some letter names and shapes, including the letters in the child's name.

◆ Begin to demonstrate reading-like behaviors, such as pretending to read and write.

◆ Begin to demonstrate understanding of picture books and simple stories.

◆ Retell stories, make predictions, and connect stories to background experiences in a teacher-guided group format.

Although comparable expectations for mathematics learning are not available, suggestions for prekindergarten expectations can be found. Shane (1999) states, "Preschool mathematics programs offer a wealth of ideas and experiences to promote the construction of mathematical concepts"; for example, methods emphasizing verbalization, reflection, and the use of real objects are essential to mathematics learning.

CHAPTER 3

The Preschool Child

F ROM AGES THREE THROUGH FIVE, CHILDREN DEVELOP INCREASED MASTERY of language and begin to think symbolically and logically. These developments allow them to observe, investigate, and engage with the physical and social environment in new ways. Preschool-age children's development of gross and fine motor skills enables them to move confidently through space; manage finer, more complex tasks; and take more care of personal needs, such as going to the toilet and getting dressed.

Culture, age, and individual differences affect the learning and development of the preschool-age child. Typically developing children of the same age vary widely in their mastery of various social, cognitive, and physical skills; nevertheless, identified progressions of skill development are common to all children. The young three-year-old is markedly different from the five-year-old across all developmental domains. Most three-year-olds are more interested in free play, for example, than in organized games with rules; whereas five-year-olds begin to want the challenge of more structured games that involve strategies and rules. Most three-year-olds are more concerned with the *process* of creating a clay object or painting a picture than with the finished *product;* whereas many five-year-olds are working toward a preconceived and preplanned end product that they want to keep or show to others. Most three-year-olds are not too concerned with the line between what is imaginary and what is real; many five-year-olds ask whether a play activity is real or "just pretend" to decide whether and how they want to engage in the activity.

Social Development

One of the major tasks for children in preschools is learning to form independent relationships of trust with adults outside the family. Children from ages three through five become more conscious that the role of caregivers with whom they spend part of their day is both similar to, and distinct from, that of their parents.

Also important during the preschool years is learning how to interact with other children and develop positive social relationships. These aspects of normal development in the preschool years move children away from the egocentrism typical of infants and toddlers and toward *perspective taking,* defined as the ability to take the perspective of others. Other important aspects of this development include the ability to cooperate, negotiate, and practice greater give-and-take in friendships.

Three key tasks characterize the preschool child's social–emotional development, which is supported by the child's development of language skills:

1. The preschool child must learn self-regulation of emotions and behavior. This self-regulation means learning not to act on impulse, especially on aggressive impulse. Perspective taking and language skills are essential to this task.

2. The child must learn to express feelings in socially appropriate ways.

3. The child must develop satisfying social relationships with other children and adults. During the preschool years children gradually learn how to negotiate social relationships, enter into play with others, and take the perspective of others. By the age of five, many children are capable of a high degree of true cooperation and sharing.

Cognitive Development

An important aspect of children's cognitive development during the preschool years is the ability to represent real objects, people, and events mentally or symbolically. Symbolic representation allows children to imagine a desired outcome and work toward it, to use drawings or dramatization to represent to others what they know, and to begin to grasp that written words carry meaning. In combination with improved memory, more logical thinking, and increased language skills, symbolic representation fuels overall development at this age (Wadsworth 1996).

Cognitive abilities developing at this age include such skills as the ability to describe the conversion of matter (e.g., ice melting to water), attempted explanations of cause and effect (e.g., if a plant does not have water, it will die), and observations and questions about natural phenomena (e.g., noticing that there are different types of clouds, wondering why leaves are falling off trees).

Cognitive development from ages three through five also results in a more active imagination, a creative ability that enhances social interaction and play but that can also lead to fears of imagined dangers, such as monsters under the bed. The capacity of preschool children for cause-effect thinking is developing, but they still often confuse association with cause and effect. For example, a four-year-old might reason that people get bigger because they have birthdays. Logic connected with concrete objects and actions is also developing during this time, but it is fragile. Pressed to explain or defend a "logical" relationship, preschool children often revert to sensory data or magical thinking: "Clouds move across the sky because they are following me" (Cole and Cole 1993). Children this age are developing their ability to categorize objects by attributes. Three-year-olds usually can manage just one attribute at a time—for example, color. But four- and five-year-olds begin to sort objects by two attributes—for example, shape and color (Ginsburg and Opper 1988).

Preschool-age children's cognitive development also results in the capacity to set aside one's own perspective momentarily and to imagine the perspective of another person. This ability has profound effects on the social development of children because it enables them to enter into the give-and-take required in cooperative activities and reciprocal friendships. Engagement in these relationships, in turn, stimulates further language and cognitive development, which then enriches social relationships and play. In the context of secure and stimulating social relationships, skillful preschool teachers encourage and support children to build competence within their "zone of proximal development" (Vygotsky 1978)—that is, to take an intellectual or social step that would be just beyond their reach without such help.

The imaginary play of preschool children is strongly linked with intellectual and cognitive development, for cognitive learning and social-emotional development in the preschool years are highly interdependent. Through play, preschool children learn to:

◆ Observe the environment around themselves and the natural world and attach meaning to those observations.

- Begin to make generalizations based on observation, to remember those generalizations, and to make predictions based on them.

- Associate words with objects and thus develop an increasingly expanded working vocabulary.

Physical Development

During the preschool years children's physical growth and maturation are an important aspect of their overall development. Young children are energetic and need to be physically active. They use their bodies to investigate interesting people, objects, and events; to represent their thoughts and feelings; and to express their responses to literature, music, and the visual arts. They often move just for the pleasure of it.

Because of changes in body proportions, preschool-age children are steadier on their feet than toddlers. Longer, thinner legs and a lower center of gravity allow preschoolers to develop greater skill in gross motor activities, such as running, jumping, balancing, and climbing. Fine motor control develops slowly during the preschool years and benefits from a variety of activities, such as building with blocks, threading beads, cutting with scissors, or pouring liquids into containers. Senses of sight and hearing are fully developed, although young children vary in their ability to focus selectively on a particular object or sound.

As with all domains of learning and development, there is great variability in physical development among children of the same age. Nevertheless, clearly observable progressions exist in the skill development of children from ages three through five. For example, three-year-olds are generally less coordinated in jumping or walking a balance beam than are five-year-olds, and three-year-olds need more frequent rest from physical activity.

With developing physical skills come new expectations of preschoolers. Teachers and parents increasingly expect children to perform a variety of self-help activities independently. These include going to the toilet or getting dressed. Preschoolers also begin to assume classroom and household responsibilities, such as helping to serve food and picking up toys. Because of young children's inconsistent abilities and willingness to master these self-care skills and chores, great patience is required of teachers and caregivers. The pay-off is that children become self-confident about meeting their own needs and proud of their ability to contribute to the well-being of classmates and families.

Because of the central importance of physical activity and development for preschool children's overall growth, effective preschool programs provide for regular and frequent periods of active play across all areas of the curriculum. Gross and fine motor skills and self-help skills are regularly observed and assessed by early childhood professionals as an important indicator of children's general learning and development.

The Role of Play in Children's Learning and Development

The old saying that play is children's work expresses a great deal of truth. Imaginary play is an important means of learning among preschool-age children. While older infants and toddlers engage in solitary imaginary play, such as feeding a stuffed animal or making a toy truck roar across the carpet, preschoolers engage with one or more classmates in the more complex and elaborate form of imaginary play called "sociodramatic" play. In this type of play, children must cooperate with one another to create a story and "script," assume various roles, figure out appropriate "costumes" and "props," and negotiate new ideas for the play, such as, "I know! Instead of being dogs, we can be wolves!"

Because imaginary play holds such rich potential for promoting children's cognitive, linguistic, social, and physical development, high-quality preschool programs view play as a key element of the curriculum. Children's spontaneous play is a window into their ideas and feelings about the world. As such, it is a rich source of ideas for curriculum planning (Jones and Nimmo 1994). For example, if a teacher observes a group of children repeatedly engaging in imaginary play about illness or hospitalization, she or he might decide to convert the playhouse area into a veterinary clinic for a week or two. The teacher might also read children stories involving doctors, hospitals, getting sick, and getting well. The teacher's observations of children's resulting conversations and activities would suggest ways to deepen or extend the curriculum further.

While involved in imaginary play, children are challenged to meet the language, problem-solving, and social competencies of their more sophisticated peers. When play is interesting and important to children, they are eager to learn the new vocabulary, new physical skills, and new social behaviors that will allow them to stay engaged in the play (Jones and Reynolds 1992). Many three-year-olds, for example, have not yet mastered socially appropriate ways to enter other children's play. Coaching by a sensitive, observant teacher on appropriate language for asking to join play can help a child over this hurdle, thereby opening a new arena for learning.

When teachers regularly observe and document brief, subtle moments of children's learning through play, those records can help parents and others understand how useful and important play is in helping children learn and grow. For example, a teacher might report a child's language and social development to the parent of a three-year-old: "I watched Sarah standing outside the playhouse area today. Instead of just watching the other children or wandering through their play without getting involved as she often does, she brought the children a book to read to the 'baby' in the family. They asked her if she wanted to be the big sister, and she said yes and joined right in. I have been thinking about ways to help her learn how to use her language to get involved in play with other children, but she figured out her own, very creative way to join them."

WORK AND PLAY

Most adults, including educators, make a sharp dichotomy between "work" and "play." In this common-sense view, work sheets are included in "work," and games are included in "play." Proponents of this view say that children have to learn to live and work in the world of adults, and classroom experiences there have to prepare them for work. These people grant that children *do* need to play but relegate this need to recess, gym, and playground activities. . . .

There is no differentiation between work and play during infancy, and babies learn an enormous amount during the first two years. They learn about objects both physically and [mathematically] and about people in all sorts of ways. They also learn to walk, talk, and otherwise make their presence very well known. . . .

While some play does not lead to learning, it is amazing how children learn as they play. Some of their knowledge remains intuitive for a long time (e.g., the physics learned from flying kites, the zoology learned from visiting caged animals, and the sociology picked up from watching appalling hours of television). When play becomes too easy or too passive (e.g., the card game of War at age eight), children indeed cease to learn. It must be pointed out, however, that there are many levels of "knowing." . . .

The point . . . is that many adults, including educators, fail to be cognizant of the importance of play. Early childhood educators have long been convinced of its educational value. . . . Teachers can often be heard asking a child, "Have you finished your work?" This question usually means "Have you produced observable results?" But results of what? Thinking? Learning? The question we should be asking is not whether children are working and producing results, but whether they are thinking about and learning what we want them to learn in an optimal way.

— C. Kamii and G. DeClark, *Young Children Reinvent Arithmetic: Implications of Piaget's Theory*

Creativity and Self-Expression

Whether through words, movement, paint, clay, dramatic play, or manipulation of such objects as blocks or dolls, children's growing ability to express ideas and feelings by using symbolic representation is an important milestone of the preschool years. Creative activity and self-expression are associated with improved mathematics learning and other significant gains in knowledge and cognitive development (Armistead 1996). In addition, learning activities that emphasize creativity and self-expression provide a variety of means by which children can investigate their questions about the world and represent to others what they know.

People's various preferred means and styles of learning have been researched by Harvard psychologist Howard Gardner (1993), who originated the concept of *multiple intelligences.* According to Gardner, our society's definition of intelligence, centered as it is on language and mathematical skills, is too narrow to reflect the intellectual competence and talents of many people (Armstrong 1994). Creative, self-expressive learning activities at the preschool level can provide early childhood educators with useful information about each child's strengths as a learner and enrich the learning experiences of all children.

CHAPTER 4

The Role of the Teacher

A PRESCHOOL TEACHER BRINGS A WIDE RANGE OF SKILLS AND QUALITIES TO the job of guiding young children's learning and development. These include observation skills, creativity, imagination, the ability to listen, enjoyment of young children, and the ability to identify each child's unique needs. Perhaps most important, preschool teachers are constantly required to apply their knowledge of child development, their experience with children, and their professional judgment in ways that affect the quality of each child's preschool experience.[1]

---

[1]For more on the role of the preschool teacher, see California Department of Education. 1999. *First Class: A Guide for Early Primary Education.* Sacramento: California Department of Education.

Based on their understanding of child development, preschool teachers have goals for children's learning and development in all domains—cognitive, linguistic, social–emotional, self-expressive, and physical. The effective teacher structures all aspects of the environment, curriculum, and instructional methods to support these learning goals. Whether children are learning about conservation of volume during free play at the water table or increasing their phonological awareness through teacher-directed rhyming and word-play activities, the effective teacher is conscious of progress toward learning goals—for individual children and for the group as a whole. Continuing observation of children's learning helps the teacher make needed changes in the environment and curriculum.

Understanding Children's Needs and Capabilities

The effective preschool teacher understands how young children think, feel, and reason. Cognitive development is promoted by presenting children with interesting and important problems and activities with which to engage. Experimentation, inquiry, play, and exploration are among the approaches used by effective teachers to guide children's learning. Teachers support children's development as independent thinkers by asking open-ended questions and helping children extend their thinking with thoughtful follow-up comments or questions. Teachers have realistic expectations of what young children can do and offer them activities that are interesting, stimulating, and growth-enhancing.

Because young children can be spontaneous and unpredictable, teachers carefully structure and guide the learning environment to take advantage of children's natural curiosity about the world. Throughout the day effective preschool teachers make dozens of important, yet small and barely noticeable decisions. They know when to intervene in a dispute and when to let children solve conflicts on their own. They know when individual children need time with an activity by themselves and when the emphasis should be on cooperating within a group. They are continually sensitive to what the children are doing and aware of options in guiding and directing them.

INTEGRATING PLAY AND LEARNING: THE TEACHER'S ROLE

Despite all our protest to the contrary, the public view of child care is baby-sitting. Parents and others outside our profession expect education to look very different from play. Indeed, some early childhood teachers make a strong distinction between learning time and free play time in their rooms. My point of view suggests something different, with play and learning very integrated. I believe that children will investigate and learn about the world every chance they get, indoors and out. Our job is to continually provide a rich environment with a variety of experiences, carefully observe children's pursuits, and then offer more resources and scaffolding to deepen and extend their learning.

— M. Carter, "Making Learning Visible," *Child Care Information and Exchange*

THE ART OF LISTENING TO CHILDREN

I began using the tape recorder to try to figure out why the children were lively and imaginative in certain discussions, yet fidgety and distracted in others ("Are you almost finished now, teacher?"), wanting to return quickly to their interrupted play. As I transcribed the daily tapes, several phenomena emerged. Whenever the discussion touched on fantasy, fairness, or friendship ("the three F's" I began to call them), participation zoomed upward. If the topic concerned, for example, what to do when all the blocks are used up before you can build something or when your best friend won't let you play in her spaceship, attention would be riveted on this and other related problems: Is it fair that Paul always gets to be Luke Skywalker and Ben has to be the bad guy? And, speaking of bad guys, why should the wolf be allowed to eat up the first two pigs? Can't the three pigs just stay home with their mother?

These were the urgent questions, and passion made the children eloquent. They reached to the outer limits of their verbal and mental abilities in order to argue, explain, persuade. No one moved to end the discussion until Justice and Reason prevailed.

— V. G. Paley, "On Listening to What Children Say," *Harvard Educational Review*

Creating an Environment for Social and Emotional Learning

The teachers in a high-quality preschool place a major emphasis on ensuring that all the children feel safe and cared for. They know how to create a classroom climate of cooperation, mutual respect, tolerance, and positive ways to resolve conflicts. As Lilian Katz (1993) observes, they strive to answer the basic question, from a child's perspective, of what it feels like to be in this environment.

Social and emotional learning are central to children's development in the preschool years, and they are completely interdependent with cognitive and academic learning. Young children in particular cannot learn if they do not feel safe, if they are hungry, if they do not feel comfortable with their caregiver, or if they have not learned how to play with other children. All these factors interact with each other and either promote or detract from children's learning and well-being.

Although teaching preschoolers appropriate social behavior takes time and patience, it can be one of the most rewarding accomplishments for a preschool teacher. As much as possible, the effective preschool teacher shifts the responsibility for children's behavior and interactions to the children themselves (Katz and McClellan 1997). The effective teacher gradually helps children to learn that they are accountable for what they say and do and how they treat others.

Accommodating a Wide Range of Abilities and Learning Styles

Effective preschool teachers accept that not all children will be ready for an activity at the same time. They respect each child's need to move away from an activity, approach it in a new way, or be encouraged to persist. Sometimes a preschool child who has been doing well in a particular activity for two or three days will lose focus, wander aimlessly, and want to sit or play alone. At the same time other children in the group may persist in the activity because they find it stimulating and satisfying. Essential to accommodating a wide range of abilities and learning styles is the teacher's recognition that the goal is not just to get the children to do what the teacher wants them to do. More important is understanding what children can do and need to do at any particular time.

UNDERSTANDING HOW CHILDREN THINK

A teacher in a preschool decided to try a stitching project with three- and four-year-olds, using large-eyed plastic "needles." She quickly realized that this activity required the children to understand that when a needle goes in one side of a piece of cloth, it then must come through the back to the front. Many of the children, the teacher found, could not do that. They were not able to retain a mental image of the back of the fabric while looking at the front. They did, however, create many things that were not stitching in the conventional sense. They made three-dimensional string and bead structures with various small objects dangling from them. They practiced stitching and varied their work. They learned how to thread needles and how to keep the thread in the needle. Many of the children found the idea of stitching so appealing that they would sit for a long time just trying to thread a needle. Throughout, the teacher observed closely how individual children responded to the learning task and their particular strategies.

— Student Teacher, Mills College Children's School, Oakland, California

---

Balancing Teacher-Initiated and Child-Initiated Activities

The preschool curriculum should offer a carefully considered balance between teacher-initiated and child-initiated learning activities. When preschool teachers are planning and implementing learning activities for young children, one of the most fundamental questions should always be: How much of my direct involvement, guidance, or explicit instruction is needed to make this activity the most beneficial for children's learning? The nature of the activity; the personality, skills, and interests of the child involved; or even the time of day can influence this decision.

For many open-ended activities involving concrete materials—for example, sand or water play—only minimal teacher intervention or guidance may be necessary to achieve the teacher's goals. As learning activities become more complex or abstract, the teacher's skilled guidance or explicit instruction may help a child build understanding or skill. For example, an older four-year-old who has shown no interest in early literacy skills may benefit from an engaging teacher-initiated and teacher-directed activity focusing on alphabet letter names. If a teacher notices that too few girls are working in the block or puzzle areas, she or he might augment the materials in those centers or structure a small-group activity to attract more girls to these important learning activities.

Whether an activity is principally child-initiated and child-directed, teacher-initiated and teacher-directed, or somewhere in between, there are more and less effective ways for teachers to intervene. Effective intervention requires knowledge of the individual child and the child's learning needs, knowledge of the parents' educational goals for their children, and appropriate goals for both individual children and the group.

Throughout an activity flexibility is a key to the teacher's effectiveness in meeting goals. An activity may start out to be child-initiated, but if children have difficulty in focusing, they may need additional teacher guidance. Similarly, a teacher-directed activity may not meet the teacher's original goals, but it may change and improve as a result of children's interaction with it.

THE TEACHER AS DECISION MAKER

The effective preschool teacher is actively involved in making decisions about appropriate instructional practices throughout the day. The teacher recognizes that:

- There is a continuum from teacher-directed to child-initiated activities, and different types of activities are appropriate at different times (see Appendix D).

- Multiple methods may need to be used every day to help children achieve specific desired outcomes.

- At the prekindergarten level there is great variability among individual children, and these differences have important implications for the teacher's instructional approach. Young three-year-olds are very different from older four-year-olds, and even children of the same age may differ significantly in their knowledge, skills, and predispositions.

- The child's engagement and interest in the activity are critical for learning to be meaningful.

- Effective teachers identify specific outcomes for students' learning.

- Continuing observation and assessment is a key to tailoring instruction for each individual child; therefore, the teacher has an obligation to observe the consequences of specific instructional approaches.

    — The Expert Panel, Prekindergarten Learning and Development Guidelines

Assessing How Well the Program Meets Children's Needs

Effective preschool teachers are continually aware of the effects of the program and adults' behavior on the children. They strive to create a program environment that is stimulating without being overwhelming and to develop learning activities that are challenging without being frustrating. In the course of helping children choose and stay engaged with activities, the effective teacher is a close observer of which activities are especially engaging or of the ways in which a particular activity may be frustrating for children. In addition, the effective teacher is familiar with a wide range of assessment procedures that help in understanding the progress and development of individual children and the group throughout the year.

Developing Strong Links with Families

Teachers view families as children's first teachers and seek their assessments of a child's needs, interests, and abilities. Different families and communities have different views and expectations of three- through five-year-olds. The effective preschool teacher recognizes, understands, and respects the values of children's families and communities and attempts to make the preschool environment as congruent with those values as possible. In effective preschool programs the teacher speaks frequently with family members and, whenever appropriate, strengthens the links between the home and program. The program also encourages parent participation in activities at the early care and education center.

MAKING EFFECTIVE USE OF TECHNOLOGY

The teacher is the primary architect of the child's learning experiences within the preschool environment. In the planning stages of technology integration, the teacher should define the criteria for hardware and, more important, software and web site selection based on the preschool program's learning objectives and goals (Clements 1994). For example, sound and voice capabilities are important in hardware selection because of young children's learning needs. Selection of software and web sites should be aligned with the child's stage of learning (Haugland and Shade 1990).

In the implementation stage teachers orchestrate the children's use of technology in the routine of the preschool program. They are aware that an overreliance on computers may divert children from hands-on, language-rich, and socially challenging activities. Some important questions to ask are:

- Is the use of computers a separate, stand-alone event or an integral part of the learning environment?

- Are the software or web sites central, supplemental, or independent of the preschool curriculum?

- Is the use of technology an independent or a collaborative activity—or both?

Technology should be a regular, normal part of the preschool environment. The more integral technology is, the more opportunities it provides for expanding the teacher's role.

— The Expert Panel, Prekindergarten Learning and Development Guidelines

This section (Part 1, "Background") has presented information about the broader environment in which program guidelines about prekindergarten learning and development operate. The section that follows presents guidelines for high-quality preschool programs.

PART TWO
Guidelines

CHAPTER 5

Program Foundations

THIS SECTION PRESENTS TWO DISTINCT CATEGORIES OF GUIDELINES. THE first category, "Program Foundations," applies to the entire program—for example, addressing cultural diversity and planning the environment of the preschool. The second category, "Curriculum," contains guidelines related to specific content areas. The rationale and program characteristics and activities are discussed for each guideline.

Planning the Preschool Environment

Considerable research over the past 15 years has provided clear documentation of the effects of the quality of the classroom environment (e.g., University of Colorado 1995; Frede 1995). Results shown to relate to the quality of preschool environments include cognitive development, social skills, classroom behavior, and language development.

Environmental considerations are important in every facet of the early childhood program. Early childhood teachers and program directors refer to such well-established checklists as the *Early Childhood Environment Rating Scale* (Harms, Clifford, and Cryer 1998) or the *Classroom Practices Inventory* (Hyson, Hirsh-Pasek, and Rescorla 1990) to conduct periodic reviews of the classroom environment. Another useful additional recommended practice is to ask parents and other professionals to participate in periodic evaluations of a program's environment. This participation can provide program staff with different perspectives and support meaningful parent involvement.

All environments communicate messages. In an early childhood program, these messages may convey the beliefs and values that program staff members have about young children, ways in which children learn, the role of families, and the importance of community. The environment creates one of the first impressions children and parents will have when they enter the program.

The environment is also a means to support learning and development goals for all children. Central to a teacher's planning and implementation of curriculum is determining in what ways the environment helps support appropriate developmental goals for children. For preschoolers this support includes a sense of autonomy and independence; the development of social skills, such as cooperation, sharing, and forming friendships; confidence in solving problems and in making decisions; and a sense of self that enables children to interact competently with their world.

APPROPRIATE "MESSAGES" IN THE PRESCHOOL ENVIRONMENT

- This is a good place to be.
- You belong here.
- This is a place you can trust.
- You can do many things on your own and be independent.
- You can get away and be by yourself when you need to.
- This is a safe place to explore and try out your ideas.

— D. Trister Dodge and L. Colker, *The Creative Curriculum for Early Childhood* (Third edition)

INFLUENCE OF THE ENVIRONMENT

An environment is a living, changing system. More than the physical space, it includes the way time is structured and roles we are expected to play. It conditions how we think, feel, and behave. And it dramatically affects the quality of our lives. The environment either works for us or against us as we conduct our lives.

— J. Greenman, *Caring Spaces, Learning Places: Children's Environments That Work*

The Tone of the Environment

Preparing the environment in high-quality programs, for both children and adults, involves responding to a very basic question: "How does it feel to live, play, and work here every day?" Personal preferences and experiences—what is pleasing, energizing, soothing, and comforting—may vary among individuals. Similarly, an individual's response to the environment is based on many different characteristics. These may include:

1. *Physical space.* Many factors are involved in making decisions about the use of physical space. For example, are there opportunities for children to move easily into and out of a busy room? Do pathways provide clear directions to children, encouraging safe and unencumbered movement from one area to another? Are routes leading to different learning centers clear?

2. *Lighting and color.* Lighting and color can add warmth to a room or cool it down. Large spaces can be made to feel more contained through bright colors and bold designs. Lighter walls or strategically placed mirrors can make small spaces appear larger.

3. *Display areas.* Children's art can be displayed in ways that communicate, "This is a child's place" and "You belong and are important." There should be a careful balance, however, between acknowledging children's efforts and bombarding children with examples of their work. Many children are overwhelmed when too much visual clutter competes for their attention.

4. *Texture.* Children are responsive to environments that offer variety. Floor coverings, toys, materials, furniture, animals, and foods all contribute to heightening children's awareness of the world around them.

5. *Auditory surroundings.* How do children experience the sound levels in a room? Are quiet activities planned in proximity to one another, or is the reading area next to the manipulatives area? Some children may be highly sensitive to noise, and it may be difficult for them to concentrate or to distinguish important sounds from unimportant ones. Children need opportunities to make noise and experiment with sound and to experience the use of sound to soothe, relax, or make a transition to other activities.

In many ways the program environment can be thought of as a "second teacher," helping to structure children's experiences and to support routines throughout the day. A well-designed classroom environment also helps to limit disorganization and conflict by contributing to children's abilities to attend and focus on specific activities and experiences. This environment allows adults more opportunities to interact positively with children as they play and learn.

GUIDELINES

1 The environment is safe and comfortable for children and adults.

One of the highest priorities for families in selecting a preschool program is to have the environment they have chosen meet high standards for health and safety. California has its own licensing requirements to ensure the safety of children in early childhood programs. Many programs go beyond minimum state requirements to ensure children's safety and the prevention of accidents and injuries. Safety guidelines are readily available and should be used routinely because circumstances may change within a program (American Public Health Association and American Academy of Pediatrics 1992; American Academy of Pediatrics 1987; Cohen and others 1996). Planning, implementing, and monitoring programs to ensure the well-being of children also involve establishing routines and procedures that take into account the age and developmental maturity of the children. Evaluation of the environment should also consider children's individual needs. Do some children have specific health or developmental problems? Are modifications required in setting up a room or establishing routines? For example, the staff may require some additional training on procedures for meeting the specialized health care needs of a child who has a health impairment or the need for special physical accommodations.

Considerations of health and safety are embedded in every aspect of a preschool program. Some examples include performing routine caregiving practices (e.g., washing hands, using gloves, washing toys), providing safe and age-appropriate toys, and developing program policies and procedures for various health concerns (e.g., dealing with sick children, infectious diseases, lice). Of particular note is the monitoring of safety in the outdoor environment. Because young children are active explorers and enjoy the challenges of practicing new motor skills and competencies, all equipment and climbing apparatuses should be carefully inspected and in good repair. Staff should be proactive in their planning to prevent injuries and accidents. Three- through five-year-olds must also be guided in the safe use of outside toys and climbing equipment.

Program Characteristics and Activities

- Adult supervision is provided in all areas at all times.

- Low-level room dividers are used so that adults can easily observe children engaged in activities.

- Adults supervise children more closely when potentially dangerous activities are involved (e.g., cooking, woodworking, climbing, or playing on the swings).

- Regular health and safety checks are conducted, and all staff are routinely given updated information.

- All equipment and materials are in good repair and have no missing parts.

- The size of the equipment is appropriate for the ages and sizes of the children.

- Classroom procedures are strictly adhered to (e.g., cleaning materials are locked and out of children's reach, and potentially hazardous tools or equipment are placed out of the reach of children and used only with appropriate supervision).

- Individual needs of children are considered, and modifications to meet those needs or training of staff or both are in place.

BEST PRACTICES FOR SUPPORTING SAFETY

To support safe practices, early care and education programs should provide the following:

1. Written policies and procedures relating to accident prevention

2. Periodic training for staff relating to safety issues and accident prevention

3. An emergency plan and policies, procedures, and training to cover emergencies, such as fire, earthquake, or other natural disasters

4. An emergency care plan for each child

5. A general transportation plan and an emergency transportation plan

6. Staff who are competent to assess an injury and to provide basic first aid and CPR

7. Consultants who can recommend environmental adaptations that will enhance the safety of all children, including children with special health care needs or disabilities

8. Periodic training regarding signs and symptoms of child abuse and neglect as well as reporting procedures

9. An incident, accident, and injury report form that provides information for an injury log with specific information about the date and time of each accident, who was involved, what happened, who was notified, and what follow-up measures and steps were taken to prevent recurrence

— Adapted from California Institute on Human Services, *Health and Safety Considerations: Caring for Young Children with Exceptional Health Care Needs*

BEST PRACTICES FOR PREVENTING DISEASE

To help in preventing disease, early care and education programs should provide the following:

1. Information on immunization for all children and staff

2. Identification and protection of children and staff who are at high risk if exposed to infectious diseases

3. A systematic morning health check of children and staff and exclusion of any individual who has an acute, contagious disease

4. Strict hand-washing policies, procedures, and training

5. Routine environmental cleaning and sanitizing practices

6. Strict universal precautions, policies, procedures, and training

— Adapted from California Institute on Human Services, *Health and Safety Considerations: Caring for Young Children with Exceptional Health Care Needs*

2 The environment is arranged to maximize learning, facilitate movement, minimize distractions, and organize children's play.

Young children need an environment that is carefully and thoughtfully organized. This statement does not mean that the environment should be rigid or overly neat, but that, from a child's perspective, it should be understandable and functional. Greenman (1988) suggests that "order for order's sake is often mere tidiness and control." A preferable approach is to consider the learning goals, values, and developmental needs of the children. If, for example, autonomy and independence are desired, toys and materials should be stored and displayed in ways that encourage independent use. Similarly, materials can be introduced and made available to meet learning goals throughout the year. In the High/Scope curriculum (Hohmann and Weikart 1995), a developmentally based approach to early childhood education, the processes of understanding classification and serialization begin early in the year with simple sorting or classifying and move to more complex tasks as the year progresses.

Teachers can also use labeling as a means of helping children to make choices and to communicate where things belong. Using drawn outlines of objects and displaying pictures, photographs, signs, and words (including languages other than English, when appropriate) are ways in which to incorporate labeling into the environment.

The use of interest areas is one of the best ways to organize an overall classroom environment. An interest center is a defined area or space containing materials that may be used independently or in combination with each other around a central theme or function. One advantage of developing centers or interest areas is that dividing a large space encourages small groupings. Interest areas also support emerging social skills by providing opportunities for children to work together, share, take turns, solve problems, make choices, and learn from one another.

Program Characteristics and Activities

- The program offers many different centers of activity (at least four that are distinctly different).
- The program offers places where children can play alone or take a break.
- Examples of centers include spaces for dramatic play, blocks, sand and water, woodworking, cooking, and reading.
- Some centers may be permanent, while others may change.
- For all centers and interest areas, the teacher periodically varies the materials or themes within the center in order to maintain interest and stimulate new learning.
- Each center is adequately stocked with materials relevant to the center's focus.
- Noisy centers and quiet centers are separated from each other.
- The environment provides adequate space for outdoor play.
- The children are able to move from one activity area to another without having to walk through and disrupt other activity areas.

3 The materials in the environment are interesting, engaging, and age appropriate.

Materials selection is an important element in planning. Because children do not compartmentalize their learning, a primary consideration in selecting materials is the potential to interest and engage children. Additional characteristics to be considered are materials that:

- Encourage manipulation in multiple ways.
- Are appropriate across a developmental range.
- Lend themselves to exploration of physical properties.

Managing the classroom and helping children negotiate their social interactions can be positively or adversely affected by the quantity and availability of materials. If there is an inadequate supply of materials, such as blocks, children may find themselves struggling over control of the blocks instead of engaging in appropriate play with peers. Having several dolls or puppets available in the dramatic play area encourages children's language interactions and provides opportunities for development of social skills, imaginative play, and problem solving.

Program Characteristics and Activities

- Strategies such as labeling are used to help children select and return materials to the appropriate area.

- Low, open shelving is used so that children have easy access to materials.

- Diversity as a value is reflected in and supported with familiar and culturally appropriate props and materials (e.g., the dramatic play area might include cooking utensils and materials that represent the cultural makeup of the children in the program).

- Materials that are used together are grouped in logical ways (e.g., materials for construction, such as blocks, fences, and animals; or cars, ramps, garages, and action figures).

- Duplicates of some materials and toys are provided to reduce "wait time" and to encourage interactive play. For example, several wheeled toys are available so that children can ride together and avoid arguments over who gets the toy.

- Interest areas should provide variety and support the program and curricular goals across content areas. For example, a print-rich environment supports literacy; and writing implements can be found in the dramatic play, science, art, and literacy areas.

- There is a balance in providing both realistic and imaginary props and materials—real clothing and props are available to equip the dramatic play area.

- Principles of good organization and selection of materials are applied to both inside and outside planning. As an example, the block area includes vehicles, human figures, and other props to enhance dramatic play and social interaction.

- The teacher changes and rotates the materials as the children get older and learn more about how to use them.

- Open-ended materials, such as clay and blocks, are readily available and can be used in many different ways, depending on the children's individual interests.

4 | The environment is supportive of diverse cultures and roles.

Learning about and developing an appreciation for diversity is an important goal for all young children. The preschool environment should emphasize clear messages about the importance of understanding and respecting others. It should represent people of different ages, abilities, and gender and different roles for those groups.

A well-planned environment also lends itself to cooperative learning groups and opportunities to interact with one another in positive ways. Having children achieve a common goal, such as building a block structure, or structuring activities that promote children's development of self-esteem and self-worth are important learning strategies to remember. The environment should reflect the children's world of rich social and cultural experiences.

Program Characteristics and Activities

- Books and other reading materials provide a source for discovery of differences that include not only linguistic, ethnic, and cultural differences but also those for age, ability, and nontraditional gender roles.

- Visual displays, pictures on the walls, and children's artwork represent diverse perspectives, ideally reflecting the makeup of the children's families and communities.

- Parents are encouraged to bring in various artifacts or materials that reflect their culture, either to show to children, to leave on display, or to use in learning centers.

- Meals and snacks reflect diverse cultures and traditions.

- Adults find many ways to celebrate that do not exclude children and that are based on the child's cultural practices.

- Teachers make efforts to respect and respond to a family's values and to help mediate when there are differences between the home and the preschool or child care program.

5 The environment welcomes parents and provides a place for communication between staff and parents.

Early childhood programs are primarily places for children. However, adults may spend up to eight hours a day, five days a week in that setting. Family and community members should also feel welcome and comfortable there. A well-planned preschool environment takes into consideration a wide variety of adults' needs.

Program Characteristics and Activities

- The environment is welcoming to parents, with displays depicting such things as schedules, recent activities, or planned activities.

- Space is available for private one-on-one meetings.

- Separate restrooms and storage space are available for all staff.

- Comfortable and adequate adult furniture is available in appropriate places.

- A space is available for staff meetings without disrupting the children's activities.

- Communication logs can be available for easy access if a parent or staff member needs to share information.

- Photos of staff members and a list of their names and roles are placed where families can easily view them.

- Storage areas are designated for family members and visitors.

- Photos of children with their families are a part of the room environment.

- Adult bathrooms and sinks are available to family members and visitors.

6   The environment is accessible to children with disabilities or other special needs.

Planning the environment to support the growth and development of children with disabilities or special needs begins with using organizational tools and practices that are appropriate for all children. For many children with disabilities, the environment will require a few modifications. For example, traffic patterns need to be carefully considered to facilitate transitions and social interactions for children who have physical impairments or who are unstable in their movements. This approach leads to greater independence for all children. For children who have difficulty regulating their behaviors, clearly defined activity will support their internal control. The goal is to increase a child's access, potential, and availability for learning through thoughtful organization of materials and space.

Because the needs of children vary, teachers should consider each child individually in assessing the environment and in determining modifications.

Program Characteristics and Activities

- No child is made to feel excluded from any part of the environment due to a lack of access.

- Adaptations or special procedures or both have been identified to support each child (e.g., a sand table at a height that allows a child in a wheelchair to have access).

- Indoor and outdoor pathways are wide and barrier free (e.g., ramps and wide doorways are readily apparent).

- The visual environment enhances learning through use of color, lighting, or specific accommodations for children with visual impairments.

- The auditory environment supports children with hearing or processing needs. Teachers are aware of classroom noise levels and of competing noises that may prevent nonauditory cues or signals from being delivered with ease.

7   The environment makes appropriate use of technology.

The National Association for the Education of Young Children's (NAEYC's) (1996) position statement on technology and young children suggests that computers in the early learning environment should "be used in ways that support . . . existing classroom directions, rather than distort or replace them." NAEYC identified the following ways to support the preschool environment: first, use computers as part of the daily routine; second, choose software that enriches or extends the curriculum or learning activities. Assistive technology—defined by the Individuals with Disabilities Education Act (IDEA) as "any item, piece of equipment, or product, whether acquired commercially off the shelf, modified, or customized, that is used to increase, maintain, or improve functional capabilities of individuals with disabilities"—enables children with disabilities to bridge the barriers that may interfere with their ability to interact with others, participate in activities, or demonstrate their knowledge and understanding of their world. As programs expand their curriculum to include computer-based activities, the use of assistive technology will help to maximize the opportunities for all children to access and participate in the curriculum.

Program Characteristics and Activities

- Teachers are informed about technology and its use in intervention.
- Teachers consider the child's characteristics and needs, parents' wishes, potential contextual influences, and available resources . . . there should be a good match between the child's developmental and functioning levels, the intended tool, and the targeted educational outcomes (Langone, Malone, and Kensley 1999).
- Technology is integrated appropriately within the preschool environment.
- The staff and children not only make use of technology when it enhances other learning, but they also strive to achieve a balance in the use of technology and other instructional aids.
- Teachers understand that most children are not nearly as skeptical about technology as are the adults to whom the children's development and education have been entrusted.

Addressing Cultural Diversity

Children in California schools come from a wide variety of religious, ethnic, linguistic, and socioeconomic backgrounds. Encouraging all children to value and respect the differences—and also the similarities—among groups and individuals should be a primary goal of every preschool classroom.

The Culture of Families and Communities

Effective prekindergarten settings reflect the importance of each child's cultural background, acknowledging and building on families' cultural experiences and cultural rules for living. Teachers understand the fundamental security children derive from being a part of a community and use that cultural base to strengthen children's sense of self and feeling of connection to others. Teachers demonstrate an active interest in and acceptance of children's cultural backgrounds, and they consciously avoid and discourage actions that demean or denigrate children's culture and community.

Families from all cultural backgrounds share a desire to see their children develop the social and cognitive skills that will ensure a stable economic future (e.g., Goldenberg and Gallimore 1995). Because of economic and political circumstances, however, children's access to resources is not equitably distributed. This inequity is particularly true for communities of color and new immigrants (Valdés 1996). Often multiple teaching approaches will be needed to afford equal opportunity for learning to all children.

BUILDING RESPECT FOR DIVERSITY

In order to create positive change for children in our communities, people of different races and cultures must begin to promote the mutual understanding and respect that are at the core of multiculturalism. To do this, there must be awareness of each other's existence, perspectives, feelings, needs, and talents. With such awareness, we can then begin to seek understanding of how we are different, alike, and why. Promoting understanding and respect is a key component of building nurturing environments in which children can flourish.

— African American Early Childhood Resource Center, *Resources to Build Diverse Leadership*

The Culture of the Early Care and Education Setting

The early care and education setting itself is a small society with its own rules for living. The culture of the early care and education setting is always different from that of the home culture, and this difference may be more pronounced if the staff differs from the families in ethnicity, social class, or country of birth. When these differences exist, the program should strive to create bridges of understanding, communication, and commonality. The ethnic and cultural composition of the staff should reflect the cultural and ethnic backgrounds of the children. While representative staffing may not always be possible, it can contribute significantly to developing a climate in the program that emphasizes appreciation and respect for diversity. Recruiting new staff with cultural backgrounds that are representative of the children and families should always be a goal that is actively pursued.

GUIDELINES

<table>
<tr>
<td>**1**</td>
<td>**The program encourages and supports appreciation of and respect for individual and group similarities and differences, making the acceptance of diversity a theme that is central to the classroom climate.**</td>
</tr>
</table>

A basic attitude of respect for others, whatever their differences, is essential in creating a positive, accepting classroom. This statement applies in ethnically and culturally diverse communities and in more homogeneous communities.

Program Characteristics and Activities

- The teacher encourages children to talk about activities in their lives that illustrate similarities and differences in the traditions, practices, roles of family members, and family structures represented in their cultures and communities.

- All children are encouraged to appreciate and respect others and to be considerate of others' feelings.

- Children are taught to reflect on how their behavior and what they say will affect others. Fairness is a central concept. "We should all respect each other and ourselves" is a cardinal classroom rule.

- Children's questions and observations about differences are dealt with honestly; acceptance of others is encouraged.

<table>
<tr>
<td>**2**</td>
<td>**Program materials reflect the characteristics, values, and practices of diverse cultural groups.**</td>
</tr>
</table>

To align the program with the children's family and community cultures, the staff need to ensure that the materials, activities, and visual aids used in the classroom reflect the child's neighborhood and world. Pictures displayed in the classroom or center; artwork created by the children; books housed in the library; music, curricular activities, fieldtrips, and visitors provided for instruction; and the food served in the center should reflect the cultures and ethnicities of the children.

Program Characteristics and Activities

- Teachers have children bring in family photographs that show the children and their family members engaged in familiar activities. Those pictures form the basis for further exploration of similarities and differences among individuals and groups.

- Teachers encourage the children to bring items from home, such as empty food containers or articles of clothing for dramatic play.

- Teachers avoid books that present cultural stereotypes; instead they seek accurate, modern portrayals of diverse groups. For example, teachers use books that depict Native Americans living in urban communities and wearing clothing other than that worn for traditional ceremonies and celebrations. However, books showing traditional Native American communities in the past are also provided.

- Parents representing different cultural backgrounds are invited to come and share personal family or cultural stories or assist with activities that are representative of their group.

3 Whenever reasonable, teachers engage in practices that are consistent with those from children's homes.

When teachers follow the form and style of caregiving that children experience at home—for example, incorporating familiar ways of using language—those children are likely to feel more secure and comfortable in the preschool or child care center. At times cultural consistency between the home and preschool or center may be difficult to attain, or the teachers may feel that it is beneficial to introduce new strategies and practices. In doing so, culturally sensitive teachers communicate with parents to make them aware of the preschool's or child care center's own culture.

Program Characteristics and Activities

- Teachers understand that most parents, particularly new immigrant families, are eager for their children to learn English. As teachers introduce English, they incorporate the child's home language, when appropriate, to ensure that the children can be understood, have their needs met, and have the opportunity and motivation to develop fluency. In this way the early language experience of children is supported as they acquire English.

- Teachers understand that children may have different ways of speaking and listening based on what is acceptable within their cultural background. For example, in some cultures interrupting someone who is speaking is considered rude; whereas in others that behavior is acceptable (Heath 1983; Tharp 1989).

- Teachers recognize that some cultures emphasize the importance of individual initiative while others place a higher value on being a member of a group. Children from families that value individual initiative may be more prepared to assert their own opinions but less prepared to cooperate with others.

- Teachers acknowledge that cultural groups differ in their sense of the relative responsibilities of the family and the staff in helping children acquire certain skills and knowledge. For example, in some cultural groups, parents may believe that the teacher is the best person to help children learn to recognize letters and numbers or gain an interest in reading and writing; whereas parents from other cultural groups may take on the job themselves of introducing their children to these early literacy experiences (Holloway and others 1997).

■ Teachers have a clear understanding of cultural differences regarding discipline among the families served by the program. Preschool staff are required by law to refrain from any form of corporal punishment, for example, but this practice may be inconsistent with the behavior of parents and caregivers at home. Instead of judging the home behavior, the teacher attempts to inform parents about how the center approaches discipline and how that approach supports a child's learning and development.

CULTURAL DIFFERENCES: THE BALANCE BETWEEN INDIVIDUAL AND GROUP ORIENTATION

Among American Indians, striving for individual achievement is often not a part of the community's world view. Consequently, teachers create a sense of internal discomfort when they either pressure children to present answers individually before the entire class or when they publicly reward specific children—for example, by prominently displaying their names on a classroom chart. Being singled out for either reward or criticism may be cause for embarrassment. On the other hand, cooperative learning techniques that emphasize working together in small groups are much more likely to enable an American Indian child to use the social skills acquired at home.

— H. N. Chang and L. Sakai, *Affirming Children's Roots: Cultural and Linguistic Diversity in Early Care and Education*

SUPPORTING IMMIGRANT FAMILIES

Uichol Kim has studied the effects on Korean families of immigrating to the United States and Canada. He finds that, while Korean parents often report difficulty learning English and participating in society, their children become fluent in English within several years and feel able to participate fully in North American society. However, the children also report difficulty in maintaining Korean language fluency. Also, their acceptance of the North American values of independence, autonomy, and self-reliance leads to conflict with their parents, who often continue to emphasize a strong sense of relatedness and devotion among family members. Kim argues that when there is a basic area of compatibility across family, community, and schools, children are able to integrate both cultures successfully. . . .

— U. Kim and S. Choi, "Individualism, Collectivism, and Child Development: A Korean Perspective," in *The Cross-Cultural Roots of Minority Child Development*

4 Teachers attempt, as much as possible, to learn about the history, beliefs, and practices of the children and families they serve, and they receive support for their efforts from the early care and education center.

If teachers are familiar with the beliefs and practices that are a part of children's lives at home, they can better understand why children behave as they do. For example, in some cultures going to school, even to preschool, means maintaining a clean physical appearance. As a result, some children may be reluctant to engage in activities, such as painting or outdoor play, that may soil their clothing.

Program Characteristics and Activities

- Teachers talk with parents frequently about the ways in which caregiving is provided at home and about the aspects of their children's behavior and learning that parents consider important.

- Teachers obtain written information and other resources about the cultural practices of the diverse groups served by the early care and education center. This information can be provided through novels, historical accounts, biographies, films, and videos.

- Teachers visit the homes and communities of families served by the early care and education center.

CHECKING THE ACCURACY OF CULTURAL INFORMATION

Ms. Williams, a preschool teacher, read a magazine article about a study of Mexican-American parents' home literacy practices. The article provided some helpful suggestions about how to build on those practices in the classroom, but she wanted to find out whether the Latino children in her classroom shared the experiences described during the article. She set aside some time during parent conferences to talk with parents about their ideas about storytelling, singing, and reading books. These conversations helped her to determine whether the article accurately reflected the beliefs and practices of the parents in her classroom. She found that the article was a good starting point for discussion, but she gained important and relevant new information by learning about each parent's views and practices.

— Expert Panel, Prekindergarten Learning and Development Guidelines

5 Children are encouraged to recognize and develop strategies to use when they encounter social injustice, bias, and prejudice.

Whether or not children are able to verbalize about social injustice, bias, and prejudice, they learn about those attitudes at an early age. In prekindergarten classrooms everywhere, children enact and express the biases of their society—biases related to gender, race, ethnicity, social class, and disability. The early care and education center should be a setting that discourages bias and promotes acceptance of others and respect for diversity.

Program Characteristics and Activities

- Teachers understand the difference between prejudice and simple curiosity about others. Many children in preschool are learning about and experiencing cultural differences for the first time and have a natural curiosity about them.

- Teachers are aware of the distinction between a multicultural approach and one that does not tolerate prejudicial behavior in the preschool setting. Multiculturalism is often characterized by celebrations of traditional ethnic or cultural holidays, tasting of diverse ethnic foods, and so on. An antibias approach builds on an awareness of multiculturalism by "including gender and differences in physical abilities . . . and directly [addressing] the impact of stereotyping, bias, and discriminatory behavior in young children's development and interactions" (Derman-Sparks 1989, p. 8).

QUESTIONS ABOUT DIFFERENCES

When children ask questions about racial and physical characteristics or differences:

- Do not ignore their questions.
- Do not change the subject.
- Do not answer indirectly.

If you are uncomfortable, identify what gets in the way of your responding directly, matter-of-factly, and simply.

— L. Derman-Sparks, *Anti-Bias Curriculum: Tools for Empowering Young Children*

BROADENING ACCESS TO TECHNOLOGY

Often low-income families have less access to technology than do middle-income families. In addition, girls tend to have less access than boys. There is also increasing controversy over male-oriented software, particularly toward video games that promote violence and destructive behavior. As a result, software developers are increasingly aware of the importance of designing software that is gender neutral, appeals to girls, and represents different ethnic and racial groups.

An example of productive use of existing software that addresses cultural diversity is the Good Samaritan Family Resource Center in San Francisco, California. This preschool program serves new immigrant families whose native language is Spanish. The center has a number of services, including a comprehensive child development center, an after-school program, and English-as-a-second-language (ESL) classes.

In the summer of 1999, an intergenerational technology program was developed. Teenagers attending the Good Samaritan's Summer Youth program learned how to use multimedia applications to create presentations, productivity tools, creativity software, and techniques for troubleshooting hardware and software. Some of the trained youth become assistants in the child development center and in the parent programs during the school year. The teenagers support the child development teachers in integrating technology into the child development program and work directly with the children at the computer center. The young people also help parents in a new program in which parents work with their preschool children using early learning software and commercially available productivity tools, such as word processing programs.

— Expert Panel, Prekindergarten Learning and Development Guidelines

Planning for Assessment

To help parents and teachers know whether a child is making progress and to help teachers set goals for learning and plan effective instructional approaches for the program, some form of assessment is essential. Assessment is the process of obtaining information about various areas of children's development, functioning, learning, and progress. At the preschool level, assessment should be broadly focused, including children's knowledge, skills, behaviors, personality, and health. As described in this section, assessment is distinct from program evaluation because it focuses on children, not on programs or services.[1]

Types of Assessments

Assessments take a variety of different forms depending on their purposes (Meisels 1994). These forms include:

- *Screening.* Identifying children who may have health or developmental problems
- *Diagnosis.* Confirming the presence and extent of a disability

---

[1]Several sections in Part 3, "Resources," contain information on a variety of resources for program assessment, including California's "Desired Results for Children and Families," which is in draft.

- *Instructional planning.* Determining appropriate instructional and remedial activities
- *Readiness tests.* Ascertaining a child's knowledge of specific skills and information, relative to that of other children the same age
- *Achievement tests.* Demonstrating the extent of a child's previous accomplishments
- *Guided observation.* Using a developmental observation tool with measures designed for monitoring children's progress toward the achievement of desired results (For more information see Appendix E, "Effective Observation Strategies.")

One of the most important assumptions underlying effective assessment of young children is that their development is continuing and complex. Although a one-shot, easily administered assessment may offer some information about children's development, it is better to use a variety of instruments and methods over a period of time to develop a more comprehensive picture.

The Need for Formal Assessments and Documentation

Teachers frequently assess children, but often these assessments may not be done formally or documented systematically. Maintaining careful, detailed records of assessments provides a basis for well-considered judgments about children and enables teachers to analyze children's strengths and areas that may need improvement. Assessments can use an array of tools and a variety of processes, including collections of children's representative work, records of teachers' observations or interviews with children, and teachers' summaries of children's progress both individually and in groups (National Association for the Education of Young Children 1995).

THE ROLE OF DOCUMENTATION

Documentation, in the form of observation of children and extensive recordkeeping, has long been encouraged and practiced in many early childhood programs. . . . Documentation typically includes samples of a child's work at several different stages of completion; photographs showing work in progress; comments written by the teacher or other adults working with the children; transcriptions of children's discussions, comments, and explanations of intentions about the activity; and comments made by parents. Observations, transcriptions of tape-recordings, and photographs of children discussing their work can be included. Examples of children's work and written reflections on the processes in which the children engaged can be displayed in classrooms or hallways. The documents reveal how the children planned, carried out, and completed the displayed work.

— L. G. Katz and S. C. Chard, "The Contribution of Documentation to the Quality of Early Childhood Education," *ERIC Digest*

The Time for an Assessment

When to do an assessment depends on its functions and purpose. For example, if a teacher wants to find out whether a child is at risk of disabling conditions and developmental problems, a developmental screening should be done when the child enters the program. In contrast, if the purpose of the assessment is to document how well children are learning and progressing in the program, the staff will want to use a continuous, systematic assessment and recordkeeping tool throughout the year.

A SYSTEMATIC PROCESS

The Work Sampling System is one example of a comprehensive assessment and recordkeeping process for prekindergarten programs. It encompasses three main elements:

- **Developmental checklists.** The teacher observes children's behavior on a continuing basis, using checklists that provide a set of observational criteria based on national standards and knowledge of child development.

- **Portfolios.** On a regular basis the teacher collects samples of two types of children's work. Core items are designed to show growth over time by representing an area of learning within a domain on three occasions during the program year. Individualized items are designed to portray the unique characteristics of the child and to reflect work that integrates many domains of the curriculum.

- **Summary reports.** Completed three times a year, these reports combine information from the developmental checklists and portfolios with the teacher's own judgment about the child's progress to present a comprehensive picture of the child's strengths and areas of concern.

  — M. L. Dichtelmiller and others, *Work Sampling in the Classroom: A Teacher's Manual*

GUIDELINES

1 Assessment is done to benefit the children and to enhance the effectiveness of parents and teachers.

The primary goal of assessment at the preschool level should be to understand and support the child's development in its many facets. Using assessment to label and categorize children can seriously limit adults' views of that child's potential.

Program Characteristics and Activities

- Everyone involved in the preschool has a positive and constructive attitude toward assessment.

- Assessment is regarded as both an everyday occurrence and a tool for enhancing the progress of individual children and the entire program.

- Teachers meet regularly together and with parents to discuss different approaches to assessment and children's progress, and adjustments are made in the program when assessments indicate that they are needed.

STANDARDIZED TESTING OF YOUNG CHILDREN

NAEYC believes that the most important consideration in evaluating and using standardized tests is the *utility criterion:* The purpose of testing must be to improve services for children and to ensure that children benefit from their educational experiences. Decisions about testing and assessment instruments must be based on the usefulness of the assessment procedure for improving services to children and improving outcomes for children.

— National Association for the Education of Young Children, *Testing of Young Children: Concerns and Cautions*

---

2 Assessment includes multiple sources of information and is balanced across the cognitive, social, emotional, and health domains.

To fully understand a child's development, educators need information from many sources. Gathering multiple sources of information helps provide a balanced view and safeguards the child from the possible harmful effects of assessment procedures that are too narrowly focused.

Program Characteristics and Activities

- The program's assessment procedures regularly involve parents and family members as highly relevant sources of information regarding their children.

- A good approach is called "triangulation," in which several sources of information are gathered to answer the same questions about the child's development.

TRIANGULATION: AN EXAMPLE OF A MULTIPLE-SOURCES APPROACH TO ASSESSMENT

Ms. Rojas, a preschool teacher, is interested in understanding more fully why David is behaving aggressively with his peers. She obtains information from a variety of sources, beginning with the observation of David in the preschool setting. She observes, for example, the frequency of his aggressive behavior and the activities and persons that provoke it. She also speaks with his parents about his behavior at home. And she uses a structured checklist that provides indicators of social behavior for children David's age. She combines all this information into a summary report, which she uses as a basis for planning ways to help David gain self-control and find positive outlets for his aggression.

— Expert Panel, Prekindergarten Learning and Development Guidelines

---

3 Assessment takes place in a context or setting that is natural, nonthreatening, and familiar to the children.

As much as possible, assessment should reflect the settings and the types of relationships the child is accustomed to in daily life. Assessment procedures that occur outside the typical boundaries or context of a child's experiences may produce highly misleading information. The assessment process may also frighten or inhibit the child from behaving naturally.

Program Characteristics and Activities

- Testing and assessment are done in settings that are natural and familiar to the child, as opposed to unfamiliar, artificial settings structured exclusively for the purpose of testing.

- Both the child's home and early care and education center are considered appropriate environments for testing and assessment.

- Assessment that engages the child is conducted primarily by people who are familiar with the child and who understand the child's unique behavioral traits. Strangers may intimidate the child.

- One of the most important and useful forms of assessment in preschools is observation. It allows teachers to learn about children by carefully watching them, listening to them, and studying their work. When using observation as an assessment technique, teachers should:

  – Ask questions that encourage children to describe their thinking.

  – Listen to children as they describe how they made decisions and solved problems.

- Watch children as they play and work with materials and other children.

- Hold conferences with children about their work.

- Listen as children talk with others informally and during group discussions.

- Study the children's work (e.g., projects, writing, drawings).

A COMMON QUESTION

Q: How can I possibly observe everything that is going on in the classroom?

A: You cannot observe everything that happens in your classroom. To maximize the effectiveness of your observations, it is best that they be planned and focused. . . . Devising a plan about whom and what to observe as part of weekly planning makes the task of observation more systematic. Some ideas include observing:

- Four or five pupils each day

- A group of students for the week

- One domain (e.g., language arts or social development) for several days

- A few components of one domain during a lesson

Becoming a skilled observer takes time and practice. Teachers usually find it beneficial to try out several methods of observation and recording, then talk them over with colleagues and revise their plans before they create a method that reflects their personal style. Above all, it is important to try to establish a routine in which you observe and document classroom activities on a regular and consistent basis.

— M. L. Dichtelmiller and others, *Work Sampling in the Classroom: A Teacher's Manual*

---

 4 **Assessment is continuous and is used regularly for planning and developing specific strategies to support children's learning and development.**

Assessment should be ongoing, showing change and progress in the whole child over time. A variety of assessments should be done at different times to give a complete picture of the child. One child may do better in the mornings, for example, while another has a difficult time if he or she does not take a nap. A child may be easily distracted by a friend and may be able to focus better when the friend is absent. Factors like these can be determined by assessing children at varying times. In addition, assessment should provide information on a continuing basis to help teachers plan instructional activities for both individual children and groups of children.

Program Characteristics and Activities

■ Teachers regularly and consistently use a variety of assessment methods to understand and document what children do, both individually and in groups.

■ Teachers use these assessments as a basis for planning and developing new curricular and instructional approaches and for helping children to advance their knowledge and skills.

5 Assessment for admission or placement purposes has few appropriate uses in preschool; but, if it is done, it should have an established reliability and validity, and it should be conducted by trained examiners.

Assessments are sometimes used to make decisions about such aspects of children's schooling as admission to a program or placement in a special track. Although this type of assessment should be used rarely at the preschool level, even assessment for referral to special services should be approached with extreme care. Because this type of assessment has important consequences for the child, tests should have established levels of reliability and validity. Simply put, *reliability* refers to the consistency of a test; that is, does the child provide similar answers at multiple points in time? *Validity* refers to the believability of the test; that is, does the test measure what it says it is supposed to measure?

Program Characteristics and Activities

■ The examiner is trained not only in administering the test but also in understanding young children's behavior during test taking when formal measures are employed for assessment.

■ Skilled examiners understand the range of a child's attention span, including a child's desire to terminate a test.

■ Skilled examiners have alternative, developmentally appropriate means of assessment, such as observing the child in play, when young children have difficulty in taking a standardized test.

ASSESSMENT INSTRUMENTS THAT REFLECT SOUND PRINCIPLES OF CHILD DEVELOPMENT

Under pressure to produce quick formulations or "scores," professionals have often called on their experiences with procedures and instruments developed for assessing selected competencies and skills in older children. These procedures and instruments can often yield misleading information. They are not built on a model of how the infant and young child develop within the family; they do not reflect an understanding of the specific types of difficulties and developmental challenges that children and families face. . . ; and they do not represent the best ways to observe and assess the dynamic development process as it occurs in infancy and early childhood.

> — S. I. Greenspan and S. J. Meisels, "Toward a New Vision for the Developmental Assessment of Infants and Young Children," in *New Visions for the Developmental Assessment of Infants and Young Children*

6 Programs direct significant efforts toward developing assessments that are accurate, fair, and free of cultural bias.

In preschool programs special care should be taken with assessments that require significant linguistic processing or language-based responses. Test procedures and processes should be culturally, linguistically, and developmentally fair. Observational or nonverbal approaches should also be used. In addition, those who perform language assessment should keep in mind the child's home language and seek to identify growth and strength with both English and the home language.

Program Characteristics and Activities

- Children who do not speak English as their primary language, or who have been raised in different cultures, are assessed with instruments that reflect their language and culture.

- The program seeks out alternative forms of assessment that take into account children's linguistic development and cultural orientation.

- The program's assessment procedures include a variety of assessment instruments and approaches that take cultural, linguistic, and developmental differences into account.

- The assessment process takes into account the possibility of biases when assessment instruments or procedures do not take the child's home language or culture into consideration (Bondurant-Utz 1994).

7 **As much as possible, parents are aware of and involved in assessments of their children.**

Parents need to be fully informed and aware of the different kinds of assessments being done in the early care and education setting. Information about the child's behavior at home and in other places outside the early care and education setting should be sought from parents because this knowledge can be helpful with program-based assessments.

Program Characteristics and Activities

- The program regularly provides parents with information about the kinds of assessments that are being conducted.

- Teachers confer periodically with parents to discuss their child's progress and other results of assessments.

- Teachers actively enlist parental support and participation in assessment procedures when appropriate.

USING TECHNOLOGY IN ASSESSMENT

Certain unique features of technology can be useful for recording information collected as a part of the assessment process. These include:

- Easy storage and retrieval of assessment data

- Capabilities of tracking to maintain assessment data of individual preschool children over time

- Capabilities of data analysis to manipulate, aggregate, and analyze assessment data in different ways

- Capabilities of reporting to integrate, synthesize, and customize assessment results in a variety of different formats; for example, the ability to create assessment reports that can satisfy program requirements or provide feedback to parents

Early learning software should always have built-in assessment features; for example, the capability of tracking the performance of children as they use individual software activities within a given software application.

— Adapted from High/Scope Educational Research Foundation, *Child Observation Record*

Including Children with Disabilities or Other Special Needs

The purpose of this section is to provide a broad framework for early childhood educators that will help in planning and implementing quality educational programs for the inclusion of young children with disabilities or other special needs in regular early care and education settings. Program approaches for children who do not qualify for special educational services but who have such special needs as behavioral or attentional problems are also offered.

For an overview of California's system for delivering services to children with disabilities or other special needs, see Appendix F, "Special Needs Legislation and Services," and Appendix G, "Map to Services for Children with Special Needs and Their Families."

Inclusion as a Program Goal

Over the past 30 years, changes in both state and federal laws and in public policies and attitudes have resulted in growing numbers of young children with disabilities and other special needs participating with typically developing peers in early care and education settings. Inclusion of children with disabilities or other special needs brings both benefits and challenges to the early childhood setting. To ensure that all children, including those with special learning or developmental needs, have access to quality educational programs requires collaboration, flexibility, and the willingness to change on the part of children, parents, teachers, specialists, and administrators. Additional adaptations may be required in the planning of the daily environment, curriculum, and instructional practices and in the management and implementation of a program to ensure that the individual goals for all children are met.

The concept of "inclusion" or "an inclusive educational program" may vary across communities and program settings. However, it generally describes qualities of programs in which:

- ◆ The educational goals for a child with a disability or other special needs are met in typical early childhood settings to the greatest extent possible.

- ◆ A child with a disability or other special needs has access to and participates in the general curriculum and activities.

- ◆ Supports and services are available to the early childhood education staff to help them best meet the individual needs of a child with a disability or other special needs.

Inclusion as an overarching program goal supports the growth and development of all children. This statement is particularly true when educators hold themselves accountable for the progress of all children, including those with diverse learning or developmental needs. When thoughtfully planned and implemented, inclusive programs contribute to a sense of community within early childhood settings by creating places where all families and children belong. Research indicates that the most effective programs are those in which all collaborators (families, early childhood educators, special educators,

and administrators) have shared values and goals for including children with disabilities or other special needs. Inclusion is understood to benefit all children, families, and communities.

Services for Children with Other Special Needs

Some preschool-aged children have special needs that do not meet the eligibility criteria for special education services but that nonetheless require modifications or adaptations to the environment, curriculum, or instructional strategies so that those children may function successfully in the classroom. Such adaptations may include providing left-handed scissors, establishing eye contact with a child before speaking, or identifying community resources to help families.

An area of increasing concern in early childhood education is providing responsive and caring environments for children with behavioral concerns. Young children communicate their well-being through their behaviors. Difficult behavior often indicates that a child is experiencing stress that may result from a number of factors, such as fatigue, poor nutrition, illness, pain, or discomfort. A child may be stressed due to an absent or ill family member or to other disruptions in the home. Most children are able to handle stress over a short period of time. This statement is particularly true when children have consistent and supportive caregivers. However, for some children, the inability to deal with stress may be communicated through challenging behaviors that are frequent, persistent, or extreme.

Unfortunately, there are increasing numbers of children who are at risk in their development, but who are not eligible for support services. Early childhood educators have two general goals for such children: (1) to provide an environment where the child feels safe, secure, and cared for; and (2) to help the child deal with stress in ways that interfere as little as possible with learning and development.

CAREGIVING STRATEGIES FOR BUILDING RESILIENCY

Caregivers may find the following information useful in building resiliency in children:

1. Children are at risk to the extent that they have not developed the self-esteem and skills needed to handle everyday stresses, to the extent that they have poorly organized or immature nervous systems, and to the extent to which their family and child care situations are stressful. Children indicate that their stresses are overwhelming when their behavior is consistently out of bounds.

2. It is important that caregivers interpret most negative behavior as an inability to cope rather than as an indicator of "willfulness" or defiance. Children prefer to deal with their world in effective ways.

3. Every child has strengths and feelings that need to be acknowledged.

4. All children need help in dealing with stressful life events, such as separations, divorce, illness, and death. Providers help when they discuss such events in an age-appropriate manner with the child, put words to the feelings that the child is experiencing, and offer reassurance and support to the child.

5. Many children need to be taught and re-taught appropriate ways to express anger, disappointment, frustration, fear, and sadness. They need support in resolving their conflicts.

6. An effective way to help children cope with stress is to build on their sense of self-mastery.

7. Additional tips for attentive caregiving follow:

   • Develop a mutually respectful relationship with a child's parents.

   • Learn about the child's birth, social, medical, and developmental history.

   • Ask parents to inform you of past and present family events that might influence the child's sense of self and stress levels.

   • Keep a log of the child's behavior to identify "triggers" and patterns of stress in the child's life.

   • Share observations of the child's progress and other developmental concerns with the parents.

   • Identify the environmental and interactional stresses the child is experiencing and the supports you can provide as a caregiver.

   • Identify resources within your community that can further help children and families.

   — Adapted from M. K. Poulsen, "Caregiving Strategies for Building Resilience in Children at Risk," in *Project EXCEPTIONAL: A Guide for Training and Recruiting Child Care Providers to Serve Young Children with Disabilities*

According to the Council for Exceptional Children (1993), many types of interventions and strategies are available to address challenging behaviors in young children. Those approaches include, but are not limited to:

◆ Assessing whether adult behavior toward children may be maintaining a child's challenging behavior (e.g., giving a child a cookie when he or she screams)

◆ Designing environments and activities to prevent challenging behavior

- Using effective positive behavioral interventions that address both the form and the function of challenging behavior

- Adopting strategies for curricular modification and accommodation to help children learn behaviors appropriate to their settings

- Seeking external consultation and technical assistance or additional staff support

- Providing opportunities for all professionals who work with children in implementing individualized education programs or individualized family service plans to acquire the knowledge and skills necessary to implement effective prevention and intervention programs

As is the case with children with disabilities, children with other types of special needs must be assessed systematically and regularly so that staff members are aware of each child's progress toward goals and so that intervention is timely if problems or concerns arise. In high-quality early care and education programs, staff members receive professional development and training in areas of disabilities and other special needs. Staff members are also aware of community resources available to children with special needs and their families.

GUIDELINES

1 | **Teachers accept and actively support the concept of inclusion by creating a classroom environment in which all children and families feel that they are welcome.**

Teachers in high-quality preschool programs regard children with disabilities or other special needs as children first and as children with special needs second. The child's individual personality, learning strengths, needs, and interests are taken into account in setting learning goals and planning activities. Likewise, families of children with special needs are viewed as having the same kinds of concerns for their child's well-being and progress as do families of typically developing children. With the resources, technical assistance, and support necessary to adapt curriculum, instruction, and assessment, teachers can successfully include children with disabilities or other special needs. Inclusion has positive benefits not only for those children and their families but also for typically developing children in the program, who learn about acceptance and appreciation of individual differences (Bailey and others 1998; Bricker 1978; Buysse and Bailey 1993; Hundert and others 1998; Lamorey and Bricker 1993; Odom and Diamond 1998; Scruggs and Mastropieri 1996; and Wolery and Wilbers 1994).

Program Characteristics and Activities

- Teachers are aware of and comply with all aspects of federal and state laws that pertain to children with disabilities.

- All children and adults in the classroom welcome and support children with disabilities or other special needs.

- Teachers actively encourage acceptance of children with disabilities or other special needs and positive social interactions among all children through adaptation of the environment, curriculum, and instructional practices.

- Children with disabilities and other special needs are regularly provided with opportunities to develop friendships with other children in the classroom.

FINDING DAYCARE FOR ROBERT

The other children in his daycare have accepted Robert as one of the gang. When I bring him over, many of them simply say, "Robert's here . . . Hi, Robert!" This acceptance brings tears to my eyes. It means so much to me to know that my son has *friends*. They know he is different and ask the provider many questions, but they talk to him and play with him like he is one of them. I believe that Robert is learning from the other children and the other children are learning at a very early, tender age to accept others for who they are despite their disabilities.

— California Department of Education, "Finding Daycare for Robert," *Bridges*

---

2 | **Teachers are a part of the educational team that develops and implements individualized education programs (IEPs) for children eligible to receive special education services.**

Children over the age of three who qualify for special education must have an IEP developed by an interdisciplinary team. As required by federal and state laws, the IEP contains clearly identified goals and objectives that are regularly monitored. (See Appendix F, "Special Needs Legislation and Services," for more information.) This team includes the child's parents or guardians; the prekindergarten teacher, as required by the federal Individuals with Disabilities Education Act (IDEA); special education professionals; and the child. The emphasis on a cooperative team approach has numerous potential benefits, including mutual support and communication. Regular classroom and curricular routines and activities for many children with disabilities will require a minimal degree of modification. For example, the program might already be serving children who have a language delay or a learning disability.

The team can support the early childhood staff in helping to meet the goals and individual needs of the child within the early care and education setting. Cooperative teams can also help establish a practice of staff planning and implementing curricula to meet the needs of all children.

ROLE OF THE REGULAR TEACHER AS A PART OF THE IEP TEAM

The role of the regular teacher as a part of the IEP team is to:

- Provide information and observations about a child's strengths and needs.
- Provide information about the general curriculum.
- Identify needed supplementary services and aids.
- Identify needed program modifications.
- Identify needed support for program personnel.
- Develop recommendations for interventions.

Program Characteristics and Activities

- As much as possible, teachers integrate approaches for helping children with disabilities or with other special needs into their regular daily classroom routines and practices. For example, a child's IEP may include regular peer interaction as a means to promote the development of language skills. In this case, adults might introduce strategies that promote child-to-child communication throughout the day, such as extending conversation, asking questions, or helping to interpret children's communication.

- Other parts of the IEP may consist of the teacher following an instructional approach that is used with all children in the classroom. For example, for children with low vision, a teacher needs to provide more verbal directions and information instead of requiring children to rely on visual information. This strategy is helpful for all children's understanding because it provides additional information and direction.

SEVEN PRIMARY GOALS FOR THE EDUCATION OF YOUNG CHILDREN WITH DISABILITIES AND OTHER SPECIAL NEEDS

Seven primary goals for educating young children with disabilities and other special needs are listed as follows:

1. Supporting families in achieving their own goals
2. Promoting child engagement and mastery
3. Promoting development in important areas
4. Building and supporting social competence
5. Facilitating the generalized use of skills
6. Providing and preparing for normalized life experiences
7. Preventing future problems or disabilities

— D. B. Bailey and M. Wolery, *Teaching Infants and Preschoolers with Disabilities*

3 Teachers work collaboratively with other specialists to determine appropriate modifications in the curriculum, instructional methods, or classroom environment.

Children with disabilities and other special needs often require modifications in educational environments or instructional activities. Many of these children may also require specialized therapeutic services. Sometimes these services are provided directly by a specialist, such as a speech-language pathologist, an occupational therapist, or a physical therapist. Sometimes classroom and instructional modifications are recommended by the parent or other consultants. The most effective practice occurs when staff and family members work together.

Early childhood educators sometimes need to be reminded of their own skills and knowledge about children and ways in which they can contribute to an effective team effort involving teachers, families, and specialists.

Program Characteristics and Activities

- The teacher, parent, and specialist plan together to modify the curriculum according to the requirements of the child's IEP. For example, special materials or equipment are included for use in the classroom, or an activity may be broken into smaller steps.

- Strategies to enhance learning and autonomy take into consideration the degree of visual and sound stimulation present in the learning environment.

- Work areas and learning materials promote children's interactions and play. Children can participate in meaningful and relevant ways independently, partially assisted, or totally assisted.

- Teachers are sensitive to the level and degree of help required by each child. Children who require more cues or prompting to interact with materials, participate in activities, or persist with an activity find consistent support from a caring adult.

- The physical environment supports children who have difficulty in moving or who use large equipment such as wheelchairs. Toys and materials are accessible, and all children can be positioned similarly; for example, sitting on the floor, standing in line, or sitting in a chair.

SUPPORT SERVICES

Support services identified in a child's individualized education program (IEP) may include the following:

- Assistive technology
- Audiology
- Counseling
- Health services
- Occupational therapy
- Orientation and mobility
- Parent counseling and training

- Physical therapy
- Psychological services
- Social work services
- Speech-language pathology services
- Transition
- Transportation
- Vision services

---

4 | **Programs provide sufficient release time, training, information, and support for teachers to plan and consult regarding children with disabilities or other special needs.**

Including children with disabilities or other special needs inevitably takes additional teacher time. To promote the success of such efforts, programs provide release time and opportunities for training and reflection so that teachers can gain the skills and information they need. Teachers report that one of their most common needs to help make inclusion effective is regular access to consultants (Scruggs and Mastropieri 1996). Early childhood teachers need information about specialized resource agencies and professionals, and they need the time and support necessary to work with such specialists.

Program Characteristics and Activities

- Professional development activities and staff support sessions provide teachers with ample time to meet and to discuss the best ways to help children with disabilities or other special needs.

- The staff meets regularly to discuss assessments or IEPs, to plan instructional strategies, and to monitor individual children's progress.

- Time to meet with parents is a high priority, and special arrangements are made to accommodate parents' schedules, if necessary.

5 Teachers work closely with families in an educational partnership and provide them with appropriate information and support.

Early intervention in high-quality preschool programs is the most effective when families and caregivers work in an equal, respectful partnership to assess a child's strengths and needs, to make decisions, and to set goals for the child's learning and development (California Department of Education 1996a).

Program Characteristics and Activities

- Staff are open, sensitive, and caring in response to initial contact by the family of a child with disabilities or other special needs.

- Staff establish trust with the families of a child with disabilities or other special needs by being consistently available, maintaining confidentiality, sharing significant information, maintaining a safe environment, and demonstrating that they value and like the child (California Department of Education 1996a).

- Special attention is given to ongoing daily communication with families. Exchanging a notebook with information about the child between the child care setting and home is an effective strategy for achieving this communication.

- Staff are aware of community resources available to families of children with disabilities or other special needs.

- Family activity days and special events are planned, and consideration is given to the needs for physical access and to the interests of families with children with disabilities or other special needs.

- Open-ended questions about children and active listening characterize staff members' communication with families to get information about children with disabilities or other special needs.

- Child care providers operate within the bounds of their professional knowledge and experience when assessing the strengths or needs of a child with disabilities or other special needs. They refer parents to appropriate specialists when they reach the limits of their expertise.

- Staff offer families opportunities to explore with other families the common interests and concerns about child development, parenting, or concerns specific to special needs.

- Staff are provided with information and training that help them address special or individual needs of children in their programs.

- Cultural preferences are explored and respected in communicating with families about children with disabilities or other special needs.

Involving Parents and Families

An overarching principle for high-quality preschool programs is that teachers build partnerships with the children's parents, guardians, and other primary caregivers.[2] They recognize and respect the family and home as the primary place for each child's learning and development (Hess and Holloway 1984; Holloway and Fuller 1999).

Ways for Teachers to Involve Parents

Effective preschool teachers strive to develop respectful relationships with parents by recognizing the parents' goals and values. They give parents confidence that their own standards for their children's development will be valued. Thus, instead of conveying information from the teacher to the parent, the teacher makes the effort to foster a respectful dialog (Valdés 1996).

Teachers in a high-quality preschool program are skillful in sharing their knowledge of appropriate learning activities for children with their families. Teachers emphasize the many ways in which children's interactions with adults at home can enhance children's school achievement. For example, children whose families read to them are better prepared for kindergarten than those whose parents do not (Goldenberg and Gallimore 1995). Skillful teachers make such strategies as reading aloud available to parents in a way that supports the parents' own child-rearing styles.

Effective teachers also promote and support family members to become involved with the school and to form relationships with the staff (Powell 1989; Powell 1994). Although teachers differ widely in the extent to which they involve families, increase their participation in the classroom, and work as partners (Epstein 1992), the commitment and the effort can help to develop that ability.

---

[2]The term *parent* is used to represent any person playing a primary role in the care of the child at home.

GUIDELINES

> ## 1 The teacher incorporates parents' goals into program instruction and supports the involvement of parents in helping their children to attain those goals.

The most successful opportunities for parent involvement are those that address the ideas of parents about their roles in their children's education and their sense of efficacy in helping their children to succeed in school (Hoover-Dempsey and Sandler 1997). Working with parents to define shared goals helps to strengthen the home-school partnership.

Program Characteristics and Activities

- The teacher begins by acknowledging that parents know their children and have goals for them and strategies for achieving those goals.

- The teacher takes the lead in making it clear to parents that their goals and concerns are understood and respected. This approach, however, does not mean that whatever parents want should be implemented as a part of the program. In some cases teachers and parents may need to confer and negotiate with each other to reach agreement on specific points.

- In a high-quality program, the following occurs:
  - Parents and teachers have regular times for conferences.
  - Teachers inquire about the child's home life and take their knowledge about the child into consideration when structuring the program.
  - Teachers regularly share assessments and work portfolios with parents.

DESIRED RESULTS FOR FAMILIES

One method of assessing the achievement of desired results for families is to seek recommendations from parents through the use of a family survey distributed by programs. The family survey uses measures and indicators to gather information from families about how they perceive the program to be supporting the achievement of desired results. Questions focus on how classroom activities are helping to support their child's learning and development and on how well the center is meeting the needs of the family. Parents are also asked about their satisfaction with their child's primary caregiver, the characteristics of the early care and education program or provider, and the types of information that have been provided. Program staff use this information to tailor their programs to support families' achievement of desired results and to increase families' satisfaction with services.

PARENTS ON THE RUN

Ideally, the parents and teacher will find time to sit down together to talk about the child's progress, go over the child's work, and exchange views and ideas. Often, however, parents and teachers find it difficult to make time for such conferences even when they want to. Informal conversations while the parent is dropping the child off at the early care and education center, or picking the child up at the end of the day, can also be productive, although they should not be viewed as a substitute for regular parent conferences. In addition, teachers eager to communicate with parents may try other approaches, such as telephone calls to the home in the evening or parent newsletters and bulletins.

— Expert Panel, Prekindergarten Learning and Development Guidelines

2   The program creates an environment where parents feel empowered and comfortable in advocating for their children.

Parents have a right to understand and request services, such as referrals to special education for their children when needed or appropriate. For parents to feel included and empowered, however, they and the staff must have confidence in each other, must collaborate effectively, and must perceive each other as caring individuals dedicated to the well-being of the children.

Program Characteristics and Activities

- An open-door policy encourages parents to visit the classroom or center at any time.

- Parents are encouraged to give their recommendations for the program's structure and content and to visit the program to observe the ways in which their contributions are used.

- Parents and other family members have the opportunity and are encouraged to share their areas of expertise with the teacher, with other families, and with the children in the program.

- Parents have the opportunity to participate in a policymaking capacity (e.g., as members of a board of directors or advisory board) in order to take a leadership role.

- Teachers solicit help from parents in solving problems their child may be having in or out of an early care and education setting.

- Parents are invited to volunteer regularly in the class and to participate in a variety of activities.

- Parents and teachers have conferences regularly, not just when there is a problem with the child.

A PARENT-FRIENDLY POLICY ON "LATE" PARENTS

The staff at Bayside Preschool were becoming frustrated with a small number of parents who were consistently late in picking up their children. Some teachers believed the parents were unaware that the teachers, too, had families to care for and needed to leave work on time. Mrs. Soto, the director, held a parent-teacher meeting to discuss strategies for resolving these concerns. Both parents and teachers had an opportunity to express their views. The teachers learned that some of the parents who were often late relied on public transportation to get from work to the center. During the winter bad weather often created long delays as buses threaded their way through congested streets. The parents expressed a concern that if they were unavoidably detained, their children were stigmatized by the angry teacher who remained waiting after closing time. They wanted some assurance that their children would be safe and occupied even if they were late. Together the staff and parents agreed to adopt a new lateness policy on a trial basis. According to the policy, one staff member would be paid to remain on the job for 30 minutes after closing. Parents who arrived more than 15 minutes late were given a small fine or asked to volunteer in the school office. Both sides—parents and teachers—left with a better understanding of the perspectives of all partners and a willingness to work toward an equitable solution.

— Expert Panel, Prekindergarten Learning and Development Guidelines

| 3 | The program regularly provides parents with information about activities in the program and about their children's learning and development. |

A key to building successful partnerships with parents is to make them true partners by sharing with them the same kinds of educational information and ideas that are important to the teacher and staff. In a high-quality program, the communication between the home and the early care and education center is continual. As much as possible, what the children are learning in the program is supported and reinforced at home.

Program Characteristics and Activities

- Teachers regularly inform parents about the purpose and benefits of the activities in the program for their children.
- The program offers regular parent education workshops that parents help to design and implement.
- The program provides a variety of information and resources for parent education in various media (print, audio, video) and in the home languages of the families served by the early care and education center, if appropriate.

BUILDING PARTNERSHIPS WITH IMMIGRANT PARENTS

According to San Francisco preschool director Greta Yin, "Getting Chinese parents involved typically entails helping them to understand Head Start's emphasis on providing children with a learning environment and the varied experiences that will help them develop socially, intellectually, physically, and emotionally in a manner appropriate to their age and stage of development." Because parents think of Head Start as a school, they often think that the structure is not academic enough. They do not understand why the teachers spend so much time playing with the children instead of focusing on reading and writing. . . .

One of the most effective strategies for increasing parent understanding of the program has been encouraging parents to spend time volunteering in classrooms so that they can observe the teachers working with their children. For example, parents often wonder, "How come my child will listen to the teacher but won't respond to me?" Seeing the teachers in action shows parents how the teachers discipline with words and reason. . . .

In part, [the] strong history of parent involvement [at Kai Ming's Head Start center in San Francisco] stems from its focus on fostering the development of the whole child within the context of his or her entire family. One of Kai Ming's goals is helping families to obtain needed services so that they will eventually obtain a higher level of self-sufficiency. Such services range from health care to educating parents or offering nutritional meals to children while they are at the center.

— Adapted from H. N. Chang and L. Sakai, *Affirming Children's Roots: Cultural and Linguistic Diversity in Early Care and Education*

ENCOURAGING LANGUAGE AND LITERACY DEVELOPMENT AT HOME

To support language and literacy development at home, the teacher can send home information encouraging parents to do things at home that will complement the language and literacy activities at the early care and education center. Examples include:

- Involving children in shopping and cooking activities, such as making lists and writing down simple recipes for snacks to make at the center

- Audiotaping a family member telling a story or an anecdote about the child's life for use at the center and suggesting that the child illustrate the story with crayon or markers

- Singing together, using a song sheet sent home to parents with lyrics to favorite songs

- Regularly sending home books for children and family members to share together

4 | The teacher recognizes the role that various family members other than parents may play in promoting children's development.

In many cases children may receive some care from a grandparent or an aunt or have most of their daily interactions with siblings, even when children live with their parents. Regardless of who the primary caregiver is, members of the extended family may be important sources of guidance, information, and support.

Program Characteristics and Activities

- Effective teachers are careful about how they refer to children's families and do not assume that all families are the same. To become more familiar with the family situation, the teacher talks informally with whoever brings the child to the program in the morning. These conversations, in turn, can lead to written communication or telephone conversations with appropriate family members and caregivers when necessary.

- In acknowledging the diversity of family structures, effective teachers do the following:

  - Identify the child's primary caregiver(s).

  - Invite all significant family members to participate in daily routines and special events.

  - Recognize that siblings or other family members may be engaging in informal educational experiences at home with the child.

  - Demonstrate acceptance of all types of family groupings and use educational materials that reflect nontraditional families.

SUPPORTING LEARNING AT HOME

A preschool teacher learned that both of Juan's parents worked most of the day outside the home. Juan spent much of his time at home playing school with his older siblings. He had already learned to recognize some letters and numbers through this activity. Another game with the older siblings, the teacher discovered, was playing cards, an activity that the teacher knew encouraged the development of mathematical thinking. The teacher used this knowledge to send books and materials home for Juan and his older siblings to use as tools for further learning.

— Expert Panel, Prekindergarten Learning and Development Guidelines

---

5 The program supports and is an advocate for strong families.

The better families are able to meet their children's basic need for shelter, food, and clothing, the more family members will be available to support their child's learning. Effective preschool programs provide support to families who want it, usually by linking families with resources in the community through referrals.

Program Characteristics and Activities

- The teacher views the program as serving the child's whole family.

- The teacher seeks current information about relevant programs and services in the community for families who need them and knows how to make appropriate referrals.

- The program provides parents with information about a wide variety of opportunities for young children in the community, such as library story time, cultural and scientific educational opportunities, and family recreational programs in parks and community centers.

- When needed or appropriate, the program provides information about educational opportunities for parents, such as assistance in gaining literacy skills, completing the GED, obtaining employment, or becoming skilled in the use of technology.

THE PARENT SERVICES PROJECT

One model of how early childhood programs can provide supportive services to families is the Parent Services Project (Link, Beggs, and Seiderman 1997). The project views early childhood programs as "a natural and comfortable means" of serving entire families through activities that seek to ease family stress. The model calls for a local parent committee to set policies, plan activities, and allocate funds; some programs employ a part-time parent coordinator. There is no predetermined curriculum; rather, the project generates activities tailored to the interests of the parents. Activities might include practical skills workshops (e.g., car repair, stress reduction), family outings with children, adult social events without children, or peer support groups. The project began in the San Francisco Bay Area and has been adopted by many programs nationally. A longitudinal study of the project found that the participating parents had lower levels of stress than parents in a nonequivalent comparison group.

— D. R. Powell, "Reweaving Parents into the Fabric of Early Childhood Programs," *Young Children*

Organizing Staff Preparation and Development Programs

Teachers attend college classes to achieve familiarity in three core curricular areas—child development, the child and family in the community, and curriculum for children aged three through five—before taking full responsibility in the classroom. In addition to recruiting prepared teachers, high-quality early care and education programs are built on a foundation of carefully planned professional development that involves all teachers and program staff. According to a major national study, preservice education and ongoing professional development can have a direct impact on the value of children's preschool experiences (Kagan and Neuman 1996).

Benefits of Professional Development Programs

Professional development can improve programs in two important ways: (1) it promotes new and continuing learning among program staff; and (2) it is a means to solve problems and identify needed resources for improving the program as a whole. Assessment of children in the program may also set the direction for staff development. For example, if children in the program demonstrate limited social development, the staff might benefit from professional development on this topic.

Professional development is also addressed when programs establish certain general conditions in the work environment to support adult learning and development. Describing a high-quality work environment for early childhood education staff, Whitebook and Bellm (1999) address four key, interrelated areas: work relationships, participatory management, work climate, and respect for diversity. Within the area of work climate, the Center for the Child Care Workforce (Whitebook and Bellm 1999) identifies the following specific topics as important for programs to evaluate:

- ◆ Collegiality
- ◆ Professional development
- ◆ Feedback on job performance
- ◆ Job roles and responsibilities that are well defined and carefully explained
- ◆ A reward system that is fair and equitable
- ◆ Involvement in decision making on important issues
- ◆ Involvement in setting program goals and objectives
- ◆ Realistic work loads
- ◆ A physical setting that is conducive to good job performance
- ◆ Encouragement of creativity and innovation

Adult development is further supported when the physical environment of the program provides for adults' needs for comfort, organization, and wellness. Eileen Eisenberg (1997) identifies four important categories of adult space in the program setting: (1) space for personal belongings; (2) planning and storage space for the successful management of classroom materials; (3) space for administrative paperwork and resource materials; and (4) areas for communication with other adults. Among the specific means she describes to achieve such an environment are comfortable, adult-sized furniture; sufficient space for the adult movement through the room; and special touches that reflect the personalities of the adult staff.

Although the benefits of professional development are numerous, they are not enough by themselves to ensure a sense of professionalism among program staff. Teachers and support staff who are underpaid and programs that are underfunded and understaffed face serious challenges. High turnover in such programs is a perennial problem that can be demoralizing to the staff who remain and harmful to children and families. A clearly defined plan to reduce staff turnover, improve the overall conditions of the program, and promote continuity of care for children conveys to the staff that they are regarded as professionals whose work is respected (Whitebook and Bellm 1999).

GUIDELINES

1 | The program has a comprehensive staff development plan.

A comprehensive staff development plan should be actively supported and implemented by the program's administrators and should also have the support of the staff and parents. The plan should be based on the assumption that early childhood educators, like any other professionals, have a need for continual professional renewal. The staff development plan should allow for a continuing cycle of knowledge acquisition, review of research, reflection, practice, and assessment of results. The plan should provide a coherent series of staff development experiences that build from one to the next, offering teachers opportunities to practice and reflect on what they learn, including on-site follow-up and peer support.

Program Characteristics and Activities

- In addition to incorporating the preceding principles, the plan should:
  - Be based on the identified needs of the staff both as a group and individually.
  - Reinforce staff capabilities in such areas of the curriculum as language and literacy, mathematical and scientific thinking, social development, the arts, creative play, and appropriate uses of technology.
  - Allow time for regular review and reflection to be built into each day's schedule.
  - Include staff relations and conflict management.
  - Include coaching and mentoring.

- Include training on the inclusion of children with disabilities or other special needs and on community resources available to children and their families.
- Incorporate continual evaluation and revision.
- Include a thorough orientation for new staff and volunteers.
- Include multiple strategies that promote teachers' development of self-awareness and reflection about their teaching, such as videotaping; audiotaping; and providing discussion groups, action research, peer observation, and visitations to other programs or sites.

- The program provides academic credit for staff development when possible.
- The staff and volunteers have at least 15 hours per year of professional development.
- Volunteers are included in staff development and orientation.

PROFESSIONAL DEVELOPMENT MAKES A DIFFERENCE

Our experience suggests that while the early care and education field may recognize [the importance of in-service training and education], some parents and policymakers do not. Parents are often concerned that more training will make caregivers "too cold," too routinized. How often have we heard that what parents want most is a loving, caring caregiver, as though training is inconsistent with that goal. We need to point out to parents and policymakers that, in fact, the converse is true. Training matters, and it matters a lot.

— S. L. Kagan and M. J. Neuman, "The Relationship Between Staff Education and Training and Quality in Child Care Programs," *Child Care Information Exchange*

---

2 The program provides adequate paid time for professional development activities.

Finding and making time for staff development activities can be a major challenge in the busy day of all early childhood program staff. Yet adequate time for planning, meeting, talking to one another, taking courses in early childhood education, and sharing ideas in both formal and informal ways must be provided for the staff to grow professionally and for the program to improve. Ideally, some staff development will include early childhood professionals from other settings, such as elementary schools, to provide diverse perspectives on a topic. Staff development activities should not be something teachers must do on their own time or without pay.

Program Characteristics and Activities

- Opportunities for discussion and observation of teaching practices are provided.

- Children's needs, both as individuals and groups, are discussed.

- Curriculum development is a part of the program.

- In-service staff development is planned at regular intervals, and staff are paid for their participation.

3 The program promotes professionalism and ethical behavior.

The program should continually support the staff members' sense of professionalism and appropriate, ethical behavior in a variety of ways.

Program Characteristics and Activities

- Teachers' and staff members' attendance at professional meetings, including presentations at conferences about activities at their school and participation in professional organizations, is supported.

- Staff members are accountable for their own professional development by regularly assessing ways in which professional development is translated into practical uses in the classroom.

- A code of ethics, such as the *NAEYC Code of Ethical Conduct,* is a point of reference and is used to guide decisions and practice (see Appendix H).

A PROFESSIONAL CODE OF ETHICS

Ethical responsibilities to children. Our paramount responsibility is to provide safe, healthy, nurturing, and responsive settings for children. We are committed to support children's development; respect individual differences; help children learn to live and work cooperatively; and promote health, self-awareness, competence, self-worth, and resiliency.

Ethical responsibilities to families. Because the family and the early childhood practitioner have a common interest in the child's welfare, we acknowledge a primary responsibility to bring about collaboration between the home and school in ways that enhance the child's development.

Ethical responsibilities to colleagues. In a caring, cooperative work place, human dignity is respected, professional satisfaction is promoted, and positive relationships are modeled. Based upon our core values, our primary responsibility in this arena is to establish and maintain settings and relationships that support productive work and meet professional needs.

Ethical responsibilities to community and society. Our responsibilities to the community are to provide programs that meet its needs, to cooperate with agencies and professions that share responsibility for children, and to develop needed programs that are not currently available.

— National Association for the Education of Young Children, *NAEYC Code of Ethical Conduct and Statement of Commitment* (The complete text of the *NAEYC Code* appears in Appendix H at the end of this publication.)

 4 ## The program provides opportunities for all staff to participate in decision making.

In most early care and education settings, it is likely that final decisions about staff development will be made by the director or head teacher. A skillful director provides leadership in collaboration and takes responsibility, when necessary, for decisions in such a way that all parties understand the decision and feel that their voices are being heard.

One of the major benefits of a well-planned professional development program is that it fosters a sense of shared governance and teamwork among the program staff.

Program Characteristics and Activities

■ All staff members should have opportunities to work collaboratively to:

- Identify areas of need for professional development.

- Solve day-to-day problems and improve their ability to solve problems as a group.

- Develop leadership skills.

5 The program provides tools and materials needed by the staff members to advance their professional skills and knowledge.

Recognizing that staff time for professional development is limited, program administrators should offer a wide variety of opportunities for staff members to enhance their professional knowledge and skills. Appropriate tools may include books, periodicals, CD-ROMs, videotapes, and other electronic media, such as the Internet and e-mail. In addition, the use of technologies such as distance learning and on-line workshops should be explored.

Program Characteristics and Activities

- Professional journals and other publications related to early childhood education are readily available to the staff.

- Electronic equipment, such as audiotape and videotape players, computers, modems, and CD-ROM players, is provided.

6 The program employs staff who meet the requirements for education and experience for their positions and encourages advancement along a planned career pathway.

California is ahead of other states in certifying early childhood professionals. All programs funded through the California Department of Education are required to employ teachers who possess "a permit issued by the Commission on Teacher Credentialing authorizing service in the care, development, and instruction of children in a child care and development program" (California *Education Code* Section 8360[a][2]). The "Child Development Permit Matrix" (see Appendix I) was the end product of a collaborative effort of the California Commission on Teacher Credentialing (CCTC), the State Superintendent of Public Instruction, and the Advancing Careers in Child Development: California's Plan project. The project's goal was to create a coordinated statewide system that (1) welcomes people into the child development field from various entry points; (2) offers clear career paths with articulated training and credentialing; and (3) provides incentives for people to stay in the field (Advancing Careers in Child Development 1999).

All individuals who hold a permit at any level, with the exception of the Associate Teacher Child Development Permit, must complete 105 clock hours of professional growth activities during each five-year cycle of their permit. The holder of the Associate Teacher Child Development Permit will be required to complete 15 semester units toward full completion of the teacher level of the permit during the five-year validity period of the permit. During the second five-year permit period, the holder will be expected to complete the requirements for the teacher level of the permit. There is no option for a third issuance of the Associate Teacher Child Development Permit.

In 1997 the CCTC adopted the extensive *Standards of Program Quality and Effectiveness for Early Childhood Education* that may be used to guide the course of study for child development teacher training programs (Sharpe 1997).

Program Characteristics and Activities

- Programs provide a clear career ladder for teachers and administrators.

- Credit-bearing educational opportunities are encouraged as a main means for staff to become eligible to accept greater levels of responsibility in early care and education settings or to find employment in other related positions over the course of their careers.

- Informal training is included as part of a child care worker's professional development. The "Child Development Permit Matrix" (see Appendix I) recognizes the role of informal training, along with formal training and other professional activities, for child care staff to meet their ongoing required number of hours for professional growth (Burton and Whitebook 1998, p. 20).

SELECTING HIGH-QUALITY STAFF

In selecting staff, [directors] need to be certain that, in the aggregate, the staff possess a broad range of educational and training backgrounds, skills, and abilities, with most of the staff having high levels of general education [and] Early Childhood Education (ECE)-related training/education and some [of the staff] having experience in early childhood settings. Moreover, directors need to recognize that the strength of early care and education is the diversity that workers bring to ECE programs and that ensuring that there will always be strong representation from the community is crucial to program quality.

— S. L. Kagan and M. J. Neuman, "The Relationship Between Staff Education and Training and Quality in Child Care Programs," *Child Care Information Exchange*

STAFF DIVERSITY AND ALIGNMENT WITH CHILDREN'S ETHNIC BACKGROUNDS

California Tomorrow [a nonprofit organization committed to racial and ethnic diversity in California] used its survey to investigate how many centers with a child from a particular racial group also had at least one staff person of the same racial background involved in caring for the children. Most white children are in centers with at least one white provider. Significant numbers of minority children are in centers where not even one adult is from the same racial background. For example, more than half of the centers caring for at least one Asian child do not have Asian staff.

Racial match, however, is only a general indicator of whether a child or provider may be from the same community. It does not, for example, detect important class differences or distinguish between the specific ethnic groups subsumed within broad racial categories. Our survey results suggest that these more specific matches may be even less likely. For example, an analysis of whether Asian children are in centers with at least one caregiver who speaks their home language shows a much lower match [for] the languages spoken by specific groups, e.g., Vietnamese, Cantonese, Tagalog.

A recommendation based on these findings follows:

> Institutions that train child care providers should also develop in-service training programs to be offered to child care centers so that those already working in the field may be informed about strategies for appropriately working with culturally and linguistically diverse children and families.

> — H. N. Chang and L. Sakai, *Affirming Children's Roots: Cultural and Linguistic Diversity in Early Care and Education*

---

7 The program has a compensation schedule that acknowledges and validates the required training and experience of each staff member.

In the Universal Preschool Task Force staffing report (California Department of Education 1998e), recommendations call for compensation linked to educational levels and experience. Pay for preschool teachers should be at parity with their counterparts in the kindergarten-through-grade-twelve system. According to the *Child Care Staff Compensation Guidelines for California 1998* (Burton and Whitebook 1998, p. 13), "most teaching staff in California child care centers earn unacceptably low wages." Many teachers with substantial college training earn significantly less than $20,000 per year, often with minimal benefits (p. 34). The benefits of higher, more equitable salaries are clear (p. 7):

- Centers that pay better wages attract better-qualified staff who provide better environments for children.

- Centers that pay higher wages have less turnover and are more successful in improving quality.

- Children in centers with less turnover fare better developmentally

The *Compensation Guidelines* (Burton and Whitebook 1998) provides a detailed analysis of salary scales by job classification, offers a strong rationale for adequate budgeting for staff and program funding, and provides recommended strategies to compensate staff fairly and equitably.

As noted in the guidelines:

> Improving child care jobs today will make a difference in the lives of thousands of California children. By offering young children better-quality care at the beginning of their lives, we are ensuring a better foundation for their future, and a better future for the entire state (p. 39).

Program Characteristics and Activities

- Adequate compensation for all staff is a primary concern of the program's administrators and parents and, where applicable, its board of directors or trustees.

- An equitable salary schedule with regular increments is a key program goal for staff development and retention.

- Guidelines for an equitable salary schedule follow (Burton and Whitebook 1998, p. 10):

  - The basic structure of the salary guidelines establishes a floor for entry-level staff and benchmarks for highly-trained staff in teaching and administrative roles.

  - An Aide's salary, which marks the floor of the guidelines, is indexed to the self-sufficiency wage required for single adults in their county.

  - The benchmark for a Master Teacher with a BA degree plus a supervised practicum is a salary equivalent to that of a beginning public school teacher in the local school district.

  - The Program Director's salary is indexed to that of a more experienced public school teacher in the local school district.

8 | Professional development activities stress the development of cultural competence.

Cultural competence is the ability to know and understand diverse cultures and cultural points of view. It is based on a deliberate effort to know and understand cultures that are different from one's own. A well-designed professional development program offers opportunities for program staff to develop cultural competence. For example, teachers may be encouraged through professional development activities to recognize that their values and cultural predispositions are based on childhood experiences and current cultural influences in addition to professional training and experiences. By becoming aware of their cultural "lens," teachers can gain insight into their practices and their responses to the children and families.

Program Characteristics and Activities

- Professional development activities encourage teachers to reflect on how their values affect their attitudes and behavior in the classroom.

- In meetings and discussions, teachers explore with each other the ways in which their approaches to caregiving are affected by their own experiences and cultural backgrounds.

- Teacher mentoring and support in programs help all teachers to develop a better understanding of the values of the children's communities and cultures and to address conflicts in values between the school and families when they occur.

9 The program supports professional development activities that focus on family involvement.

Involving and maintaining communication with parents can be a challenge to busy early childhood educators. Therefore, professional development programs and professional support should be provided regularly to help teachers strengthen and improve their family involvement strategies.

Program Characteristics and Activities

- Professional development workshops and ongoing support groups offer teachers a variety of strategies to involve parents and communicate with them.

- Whenever possible and appropriate, parents are invited to workshops and information sessions so that they have an opportunity to be fully aware of what the staff is learning.

10 The staff development plan incorporates a clearly defined approach to integrating technology in the early childhood education program.

Several elements of effective staff development (Epstein 1993) can facilitate the integration of technology into the early childhood education program. These elements are listed as follows:

- *Practical experience.* Staff development should be interwoven with practical experience and hands-on application.

- *Staff development workshops.* Workshops are effective if they include active participation, sharing among colleagues, and follow-up sessions as teachers integrate technology into the preschool or child care environment.

- *Models and mentors.* Observing appropriate uses of technology and having access to experienced early childhood teachers who use technology are both effective forms of staff development. The Internet can be used to research exemplary uses of technology in early childhood education and to find mentors through online early childhood education networks.

- *Continuing follow-up.* To sustain the learning in the staff development workshops, teachers must have one-to-one contact with a supervisory teacher, mentor, or experienced technology-user. Internet resources can make such follow-up possible.

Program Characteristics and Activities

- The program incorporates a variety of staff development elements that have been found effective in integrating technology (Hohmann 1994).

- Among these elements are:
  - *Reducing technophobia.* Basic technical skills are introduced in staff development workshops to increase confidence and provide knowledge for troubleshooting simple technical problems. Extended, successful, curriculum-oriented experiences are essential for developing familiarity and confidence with technology.
  - *Focusing on technology and curriculum.* The technology integration component of staff development is designed to fit the program's educational needs.

- Technology can also be used to provide staff and professional development. A number of colleges and universities have developed online courses and degree programs for early childhood educators who are interested in improving their knowledge and skills, becoming licensed or certified, or pursuing an advanced degree.

CHAPTER 6

Curriculum

C URRICULUM TAKES MANY FORMS IN THE PRESCHOOL ENVIRONMENT. Preschool teachers are developing curriculum when they organize the space in their environment; select toys and materials; plan the daily schedule; assess children's learning and development; and cultivate caring relationships among staff, children, and families. On this foundation of physical and social organization, teachers set learning goals and plan the daily activities and projects that promote children's development and learning.

Integrated Curriculum

Although the guidelines in Part 2 are divided according to specific content areas, preschool curriculum is often described as *integrated* because learning activities encompass many disciplines, not just isolated subjects. For example, preschool children often help prepare and serve snacks because teachers know this popular chore offers learning in mathematics, science, language development, nutrition, and social studies. When children engage in fantasy play about real-life activities, such as operating a grocery store or a veterinary clinic, similarly rich and multidisciplinary learning occurs.

Preschool curriculum is also integrated in the sense that a single learning activity may address several areas of children's development: cognitive, social, physical, linguistic, or creative. Integrated curriculum is an effective approach with preschool-age children because it makes use of their strengths as learners. It offers them interesting and meaningful projects they can explore fully with their hands, bodies, minds, and senses.

Emergent Curriculum

To a great extent curriculum in the preschool is negotiated between teachers and children. *Emergent* curriculum describes a process in which the teacher integrates children's spontaneous, day-to-day discoveries, interests, and questions into established learning goals and curriculum. With their knowledge of child development and important content areas, teachers plan curriculum to meet their goals for children's learning. In turn each child's experiences, personality, knowledge, skills, and interests determine what, how, and even whether a child will learn from any given activity. Teachers must continually assess whether a learning activity or project is sufficiently rich and open-ended to attract children with varied interests and abilities; whether it is sufficiently challenging to engage most children without frustrating them; and whether it is actually meeting the intended learning goals. On the basis of these assessments, teachers adapt activities or approaches to meet the group's and individual children's needs.

Many preschool teachers regularly involve children in the entire cycle of curriculum development: articulating a question or an idea that interests them, choosing a project or an activity that addresses the idea or question, planning and implementing the activity, and reflecting on what they have learned. Curriculum also "emerges" at times out of children's spontaneous interests or questions; for example, children may be fascinated by the eating habits of the potato bugs in the outdoor play area. Skilled teachers harness the energy of children's natural curiosity by adapting the curriculum to these spontaneous interests. When teachers incorporate children's ideas into their learning goals, children's self-confidence and self-esteem are enhanced in important ways. Children see that their thinking is respected and their questions about the world are taken seriously. Over time, such a practice supports children in becoming self-initiating, self-directed learners.

Foundational Skills

Preschool curriculum helps develop the important language, literacy, and reasoning skills that prepare children for reading and mathematics instruction in kindergarten and the primary grades. To the greatest extent possible, children learn these skills in the context of activities, projects, and play. As necessary to meet learning goals, teachers use teacher-directed or more explicit types of instruction with individual children or groups; for example, alphabet songs or games to build awareness of the connection between alphabet letters and the sounds they represent.

SUMMARY OF EFFECTIVE PRESCHOOL CURRICULUM

An effective preschool program will:

- Offer children choices.
- Provide time for leisurely exploration and for trying out of new activities and ideas.
- Balance teacher-initiated and child-initiated activities.
- Involve content that is interesting and meaningful to children.
- Involve children regularly in initiating, planning, and implementing activities and then reflecting on what they have learned.
- Reflect children's diverse cultures and communities.
- Accommodate many learning styles and abilities and offer many ways to be successful.
- Provide alternating periods of active and quiet activities.
- Offer activities in individual, small-group, and large-group formats.
- Involve staff in regular cycles of planning, implementing, reflecting, and revising.

— Expert Panel, Prekindergarten Learning and Development Guidelines

Social and Emotional Development

Young children's healthy social and emotional development supports and enhances all other areas of learning and development. Many new social and emotional skills are required of preschool-age children as they venture out into the world beyond their home and families. In the most general sense, they are learning more about who they are as individuals and how to get along with others.

A group setting is often a new, exciting, and stressful experience for preschool-age children. It requires them to develop new strategies for meeting their basic daily needs. They must learn to share the attention of an adult with many other children. They must develop the ability to wait, take turns, and spend long periods without primary caregivers. During this time children form their first friendships and learn to play and work cooperatively in groups of peers. To meet these new social challenges successfully, children must learn to control their impulses, express their emotions in socially acceptable ways, and form satisfying social relationships with others. Group settings, such as preschool, offer many opportunities for children to practice those skills.

GUIDELINES

1 The staff is responsive to children's emotional needs.

Children's healthy emotional development requires adults to be alert to children's feelings, to acknowledge those feelings as legitimate, and to respond with empathy and compassion. A child who is fearful, angry, overexcited, or otherwise "out of sorts" cannot engage in learning. Emotional support from caring adults helps children resolve troubled feelings so that they can reconnect in productive ways with friends and activities.

Program Characteristics and Activities

- Teachers express a welcoming attitude in their voices and gestures.
- Teachers are sensitive to each child's personality and ways of expressing emotions. They avoid labels and put-downs.
- Teachers show interest in what children say and do.
- The feelings of children are respected and dealt with as an important part of who they are. Talk about feelings is an integral part of daily conversation in the program.
- Teachers suggest and model appropriate ways of expressing oneself when children may not have the concepts or words for what they are feeling.
- Children hear and discuss engaging stories that feature characters' feelings.
- Children have the option of going to a "calm-down place" to sort through feelings alone or with a sensitive adult. They may remain there until they feel ready to rejoin the group. This option is presented as a positive rather than a punitive way of dealing with a situation.
- Teachers help children make connections between events, feelings associated with the event, and behaviors that may express those feelings.

2   The program climate, organization, and routine create a sense of safety, security, and predictability.

Children learn best in environments where they feel safe and cared about. A calm, organized environment with a familiar routine and clearly stated and consistently enforced rules meets children's needs for predictability in their social and physical surroundings. The commitment of children to program rules and routines is enhanced when they are involved in making the rules and when they actively participate in resolving problems that result from the violation of rules. Teachers reinforce children's commitment to the early care and education community when they explain that the rules are in place to ensure everyone's safety and well-being.

Program Characteristics and Activities

- There is continuity and consistency in the daily schedule and activities, with some flexibility based on children's needs.

- Program rules are few, clear to children, age-appropriate, consistently implemented, and developed with the children's help and participation.

- Teachers provide for orderly transitions from one activity to the next; children are not repeatedly required to wait for the entire group to be ready before beginning the next activity.

- Children are given cues in advance for transitions to new activities; plans for transitions are part of an ongoing dialogue.

- Sufficient time is regularly allocated for free play and outdoor play.

- Children's opinions are solicited regarding how to deal with problems involving rules; sufficient time is taken to ensure that all children are heard; and children are not rushed into premature resolutions of issues.

3   Each child is supported to develop a sense of self-worth and capability.

From the ages of three through five, children's cognitive development allows them to think in new ways about who they are. Personalities are developing as children strive to fulfill their individual needs and desires within the bounds of behavior deemed socially and culturally appropriate in their families and communities. In addition to viewing themselves as part of a larger group, children begin to evaluate themselves as doing well or poorly in meeting society's expectations. Preschool-age children test their own capabilities by taking increasing initiative to choose the social, intellectual, physical, and creative activities they wish to pursue. Adults support children's developing sense of self by respecting their growing capabilities, offering them choices in a structured setting, and setting appropriately high expectations for their behavior.

Program Characteristics and Activities

- Children have worthwhile and appropriately challenging learning activities to enhance their cognitive, physical, social, and emotional development (Katz and Chard 1989).

- Teachers intervene optimally, providing neither too much nor too little guidance to support children's appropriate expression of emotions and interactions with others (Katz and McClellan 1997).

- Children can choose activities and decide the duration.

- Children are encouraged in fantasy play to explore their understanding of many roles and behaviors.

- Children are recognized for achievements in a specific way rather than being praised in a general way.

 4 **Each child is supported to develop a sense of self as a valued and responsible member of the group.**

Social understanding and social competence develop in the course of children's cooperative work and play. Because preschoolers are egocentric, they often need adult guidance to understand the impact of their behavior—whether positive or negative—on individuals and the group. When teachers ask one child to be a resource for another—to answer a question, to share expertise, to help with a task—children begin to realize that everyone has something to contribute. When children see that their own behavior can positively affect the program and other children, that discovery promotes a positive cycle of growing social competence and opportunities for further social learning in the company of others.

Program Characteristics and Activities

- Each child is provided with opportunities to take leadership roles, such as teacher's helper.

- Program jobs are rotated regularly among the children.

- Children are designated to "read" picture books to other children or to provide peers with other types of "expertise" or assistance.

- Children's requests for adult help are referred to a capable peer, when appropriate.

- Children are given specific, descriptive feedback on the positive impact of their prosocial behavior.

- Simple games that foster cooperation are taught.
- Children are helped to succeed in group situations in such areas as the sand table, outdoor play equipment, or playhouse.
- Centers and opportunities for role-playing and dramatization are provided.
- Appropriate and respectful social behavior is modeled.

COMMUNITY BUILDING AT MORNING CIRCLE

Circle time is the time for community building in Mrs. Martinez's morning preschool program for four-year-olds. As part of the announcements during circle time one morning, Mrs. Martinez tells the children they will eat lunch in their classroom that day because the older children are having a science fair in the cafeteria. In the middle of the announcement, Melanie offers, "I am getting taller." Without skipping a beat, Mrs. Martinez says warmly, "Yes, you are getting taller. Can anyone tell me why it is that we get taller?" "Because we have birthdays," says Lilly. Matter-of-factly accepting preschooler logic, Mrs. Martinez replies, "Yes, Lilly, you had a birthday recently, and you turned five. We knew you, Lilly, when you were just three!" she adds.

The children listen attentively and add their comments as Mrs. Martinez points out all the children who have been at the preschool since age three and all those who are new this year. Everyone is included. Later, after children have voted on which of three possible sack lunches they want to take on an upcoming field trip to the zoo, Mrs. Martinez tells them that their families are invited on the field trip, but that younger brothers and sisters cannot ride on the bus. "The 'big office' rules say that we can't take them on the bus," she tells the children. Then she talks with each child in the circle about which family members can come on the bus and which must use their own transportation. This discussion turns into a group conversation about the makeup of children's families and a range of related topics: the difference between siblings and cousins; which children have new babies in their families; who is an oldest, a youngest, or a middle child; and whose grandparents live close by or far away.

Although Mrs. Martinez has helped structure and extend the conversation, the children's comments and questions define the content. The importance of such discussion to children is confirmed when pairs of children continue the conversation as they leave circle for free play time.

— Maria Martinez, Will Rodgers State Preschool, Santa Monica, California

5 — Children are guided and supported to form and maintain satisfying relationships with others.

Young children need guidance and many opportunities to practice and master the complex skills required to make and keep friends. They must be able to take another child's point of view, to empathize, and to understand the give-and-take required in friendships and cooperative activities with peers. Although young children's friendships are based principally on shared interests and activities, those early friendships lay the essential groundwork for adolescent and adult friendships based on mutual understanding, loyalty, and trust (Hartup 1991).

To adapt successfully in group settings, children also need to be able to form effective relationships of trust and dependence with adults outside their family. Teacher-child relationships are a major resource to children (Pianta 1998). Children's social interactions with adults are learned in their families and communities. Preschool teachers regard communication with parents and families as important in building a child's social competence.

Program Characteristics and Activities

- Teachers cultivate regular communication with each child, including individual contact and support with tasks.
- Teachers encourage contact among more and less socially skilled children by creating opportunities for them to perform small tasks and chores together.

- In the context of learning activities, teachers offer children opportunities to interact with other adult staff members and visitors from families or the community.
- Teachers provide many opportunities for children to work in pairs and small groups.
- Teachers let parents know about their children's friendships in the early care and education center so that, if possible, those friendships can be cultivated outside the program.

CONFLICT RESOLUTION

General Attitude Toward Children's Conflicts

1. Be calm and control reactions.
2. Recognize that the conflict belongs to the children.
3. Believe in children's ability to solve their conflicts.

Principles of Teaching in Conflict Situations

1. Take responsibility for children's physical safety.
2. Use nonverbal methods to calm children.
3. Acknowledge, accept, and validate all children's feelings and perceptions of the conflict.
4. Help children verbalize feelings and desires to each other and listen to one another.
5. Clarify and state the problem.
6. Give children the opportunity to suggest solutions.
7. Propose solutions when children do not have ideas.
8. Uphold the value of mutual agreement and give children the opportunity to reject proposed solutions.
9. Teach impartial procedures for settling disputes when a decision is arbitrary.
10. When both children lose interest in the conflict, do not pursue it.
11. Help children recognize their responsibility in a conflict situation.
12. Offer an opportunity for restitution if appropriate.
13. Help children repair the relationship, but do not force children to be insincere.
14. Encourage children to resolve their conflict by themselves.

— R. DeVries and B. Zan, *Moral Classrooms, Moral Children: Creating a Constructivist Atmosphere in Early Education*

6 Children are guided and supported to express their emotions in socially acceptable ways.

Preschool teachers have the important task of helping children learn how to express feelings in productive ways. Adults also help children to consider the perspectives of others, to see the connections between feelings and behaviors, and to develop effective coping strategies.

Program Characteristics and Activities

- Care providers affirm children's emotions and guide children to express them appropriately.
- Staff members encourage empathy by pointing out to children the observable effects of their behavior on other children.
- Program staff avoid gender stereotyping when dealing with children's expression of emotions; for example, telling a child, "Big boys don't cry," or "Nice girls don't yell."

A "SAFE PLACE" FOR FEELINGS

Staff who care for and interact with children daily can play a significant role in helping young children display a range of emotions and respond appropriately to those expressed by others. To do this, adults must give children permission to feel and express sadness, fear, anger, worry, and loneliness as well as joy, delight, excitement, enthusiasm, and other positive emotions. Teachers will readily convey this permission as they mirror children's emotions by identifying and affirming them, and children will represent them in their drawings, stories, and so forth. In addition, teachers convey permission through the use of modeling to express their own genuine feelings.

Teachers who allow the true feelings of at-risk children to have a voice in the classroom may fear that negative feelings will become pervasive and overpowering. While at-risk children may be full of negative emotions as the result of life experiences, teachers will find that giving these feelings a voice need not result in a depressing environment. On the contrary, children who are allowed to sing, "If you're sad and you know it, you can cry" and "If you're angry and you know it, stomp your feet!" will sing with interest, energy, and genuine shared feeling. The preschool then becomes a true "safe place" where children find acceptance of all their feelings and learn to communicate about themselves. The teacher then becomes an important link in children's affective connections, enabling children to be themselves while reaching out to others.

— Adapted from L. Koplow, "If You're Sad and You Know It," in *Unsmiling Faces: How Preschools Can Heal*

7 Children's social and cultural backgrounds are taken into account in interpreting their preferences and behaviors in the preschool setting.

All cultural groups have expectations for children's social and emotional behavior; for example, how children show respect to adults, express their feelings, interact with other children, or participate in daily family life. As preschool populations become more culturally diverse, it is important for caregivers to be able to interpret the behaviors of children in the context of their families' social and cultural expectations and practices. Ongoing interaction with families is important for teachers' effectiveness in supporting children's social and emotional development in culturally sensitive ways.

Program Characteristics and Activities

- Teachers integrate children's cultural backgrounds into all aspects of the program environment—the appearance of the classroom; the activities, toys, and materials; and the social events that are planned with children and families.

- Teachers discuss culturally defined social practices openly and in a matter-of-fact way as an important aspect of who children are.

- Teachers understand that their own cultural backgrounds affect what they define as appropriate social and emotional behavior—personal practices of others are not automatically assumed to be either "wrong" or "abnormal," nor are their own practices always "right."

8 Children's social behavior is guided in the context of daily activities.

Children are highly motivated to engage with other children. Teachers can best guide a child's social behavior in the course of real work and play with classmates. Providing children with immediate, concrete feedback allows them to learn new social strategies. This type of intervention can be especially important for children whose social behaviors isolate them from other children.

Program Characteristics and Activities

- Teachers understand child development and know individual children well enough to intervene "optimally" in children's conflicts with neither too much nor too little guidance (Katz and McClellan 1997).

- Teachers use opportunities to structure and teach social development as they occur in the program instead of relying on artificial, stand-alone lessons.

- Teachers begin the class with clearly stated standards about how to treat people (e.g., no hitting, no name-calling, say "please" and "thank you").
- Teachers regard inappropriate social behavior during play as a valuable opportunity to provide a child with new social strategies.

9 | The goal of discipline is to promote greater social and emotional competence.

When young children experience the personal and social benefits of behaving in socially acceptable ways, they are more likely to do so willingly. Teachers can help children recognize the benefits of good behavior. And teachers can use misbehavior as an opportunity to help children express their feelings and resolve problems more effectively and appropriately.

An important goal of behavior management is helping children learn to act in socially responsible ways even when an adult is not around to monitor their behavior. Using such techniques as humiliation, punitive isolation, and labeling undermine a child's emerging sense of social and moral responsibility. Punitive approaches to behavior management also damage the very relationships with adults and peers that motivate children to act in socially responsible ways.

Program Characteristics and Activities

- Behavior that threatens to harm the child or others is prohibited.
- A "cooling down" time and place are provided when children are too upset to learn from their inappropriate behavior.
- The feelings that often accompany children's inappropriate behavior are acknowledged.
- Teachers listen patiently when children explain their behaviors.
- Children are helped to understand the impact of their behavior on themselves and others.
- Children are provided with alternative, acceptable ways to express their feelings or meet their needs.
- Children's positive social behaviors are encouraged and recognized.
- Children are guided to work out differences with as little adult intervention as possible.
- The child's connection to the teacher and class is reaffirmed after an incident requiring disciplinary intervention.

EMOTIONAL SUPPORT DURING A STRESSFUL TIME

David, who recently turned four, is having a hard day at preschool. He is distracted and fidgety, unable to stay seated during morning circle. His teacher, Mrs. Gutierrez, has to remind him repeatedly to keep his hands and feet to himself. To excuse children from the circle for snack, Mrs. Gutierrez asks each child to tell her the color of an article of his or her clothing. When it is his turn, David acts silly and speaks only nonsense words. Mrs. Gutierrez tells him to wash his hands for snack time, and later she sits near him at the table. She is clearly setting the best conditions she can for him to stay connected to the group and to control his own behavior. She is patient and firm and continues to offer him choices for managing his behavior.

"David has a new baby brother at home and is not happy about the situation," Mrs. Gutierrez explains. "He has great parents who give him lots of attention, but he is having a hard time with this big change in his life." At afternoon circle, she holds David in her lap as she reads aloud to the group, gently restraining him from kicking nearby children. Soon he is absorbed in the story. Later in the afternoon, when he is disrupting other children's play, Mrs. Gutierrez offers him the option of "visiting" his friends in the three-year-old classroom, from which he has recently graduated. "When he really cannot manage, I take him to the other room, where he can be in familiar and less challenging surroundings," Mrs. Gutierrez says. As David heads happily to the room next door, Mrs. Gutierrez reaffirms his connection to the classroom and herself: "Good-bye, David. We'll see you tomorrow morning."

— Ermina Gutierrez, Darwin Center Head Start, Hayward, California

Language and Literacy Development

Language and literacy development during the preschool years has a significant impact on how well children learn to read and write during kindergarten and the primary grades. Successful early literacy learning is closely associated with achievement in later schooling, social relations, and work (National Research Council 1998).

Young children have important innate resources for learning language and literacy skills. By the age of three, children are highly capable language learners. From ages three through five, children experience tremendous growth in language. Their vocabulary grows from 900 to 3,000 words, and their sentences expand from simple three- or four-word utterances to complicated expressions using a dozen words or more. Preschool children use language to meet personal and social needs and to explore their interests. Many preschool-age children also begin to explore what it means to be a reader and a writer. An effective language and literacy curriculum is balanced and comprehensive, addressing a full range of language and emergent literacy competencies.

Society places a high value on literacy, and standards for what is considered literate are rising (National Association for the Education of Young Children 1997). At the same time concern is growing among teachers and parents about the number of children who are entering kindergarten and first grade lacking experiences that support language and literacy learning. Teachers of young children are further challenged by the diversity of backgrounds, home languages, and intellectual and language abilities of children who come to early care and education programs.

Language Development

Preschoolers are highly motivated language learners because language allows them to be intellectually and socially engaged with their families, neighborhoods, and schools. Words symbolically represent objects and concepts; therefore, language development plays an essential role in children's overall cognitive development. Children also use language to establish and maintain social relationships with adults and peers, in whose company most learning takes place.

Guidance in language development is generally best accomplished in the context of a child's ongoing work and play. Typically, preschool children spontaneously talk about activities in which they are involved or about the familiar people and places in their lives. Using a child's special interests and favorite activities as subject matter, teachers can model conversational speaking and listening skills, help children learn to sequence information, and guide them in their use of vocabulary. Preschool teachers also provide children with exposure to and practice in the use of "decontextualized" language—talk about topics beyond children's "here and now" experiences—a common strategy for introducing children to new and interesting vocabulary and concepts.

EARLY LITERACY GLOSSARY

Alphabetic principle. The assumption underlying an alphabetic writing system that each speech sound or phoneme of a language has its own distinctive graphic representation.

Phonemes. The smallest units of speech that distinguish one utterance or word from another in a given language (e.g., the /r/ in *rug* or the /b/ in *bug*).

Phonological awareness. The awareness that oral language has structure that is separate from meaning, attending to the sublexical structure (i.e., structure within words) of oral language; for example, *beg* has one syllable and three phonemes, *egg* has one syllable and two phonemes.

Phonemic awareness. The insight that every spoken word is made up of a sequence of phonemes or speech sounds. This insight is essential for learning to read an alphabetic language because these elementary sounds or phonemes are represented by letters. Without phonemic awareness phonics makes no sense; consequently, the spelling of words can be learned only by rote.

— From the California Department of Education, *Reading/Language Arts Framework*

Literacy Development

Children are born with the capacity to develop spoken language. But reading and writing are cultural inventions that children must make an effort to learn, usually with help from adults. Literacy development is a long, gradual process that begins in infancy and reaches basic competency in middle childhood.

Preschool language and literacy activities can be significant in laying the foundation for later literacy learning. Because there is great variability in how quickly and how well each child learns, the preschool language and literacy curriculum should be varied and flexible to accommodate a range of learning styles and abilities.

Decades of research and professional experience confirm that preschool-age children generally learn best through active exploration of interesting objects, materials, and events. Research also indicates that age-appropriate explicit instruction can be effective in promoting children's early literacy development, especially in the area of phonological awareness (National Research Council 1998). Several preschool language and literacy practices are associated with improved literacy learning, including the following:

- Cognitively challenging, vocabulary-rich conversations with adults (Phillips, McCartney, and Scarr 1987; Dickinson, Cote, and Smith 1993)

- Being read aloud to in an expressive manner from an appealing book (Clay 1979; Purcell-Gates and Dahl 1991; Dunn and Dunn 1981)

- Participation in rhyming and alliterative activities to support phonemic awareness (Adams 1990; Ehri and Wilce 1980, 1985; Perfetti and others 1987)

The Role of Preschools in Language and Literacy Development

High-quality preschools offer children a language-rich and print-rich environment in which to develop their language and early literacy skills.[1] Effective early care and education programs capitalize on children's inherent interest in language by providing an environment with many opportunities for interesting and purposeful oral and print communication among children and adults. With knowledge of the learning goals for children, teachers in these environments interact, guide, facilitate, and teach.

Even in the most carefully structured and stimulating preschool environment, however, some children may not spontaneously engage in important language and literacy learning activities. Children's home environments, regardless of how nurturing, may offer few opportunities for the types of language and literacy development that later schooling requires. For those reasons many children will benefit from explicit teacher-initiated and teacher-

---

[1]Detailed information on effective approaches to early literacy learning can be found in Appendix A in California Department of Education. 1999. *First Class: A Guide for Early Primary Education.* Sacramento: California Department of Education.

directed learning activities, especially those that address more abstract components, such as the alphabetic principle and phonemic awareness (Roberts and Corbett 1997; Whitehurst and Lonigan 1998; National Research Council 1999). Explicit early language and literacy instruction in the preschool setting should be regular, engaging, active, flexible, and brief, offering children many ways to participate and learn.

To support children's long-term language and literacy development, effective preschool programs create connections between explicit instruction and activities that children find interesting and meaningful. For example, when preschoolers begin to recognize and name letters of the alphabet, an effective instructional approach is to use the first letter in children's names, which is inherently interesting and useful to them.

GUIDELINES

1 | **Programs support learning and development in both language and literacy.**

In its fullest sense literacy encompasses the language arts processes of listening, speaking, reading, and writing. To some extent development of language skills and development of literacy skills are mutually supportive. But each skill area also benefits from distinct curricular approaches that address specific desired results.

DESIRED RESULTS FOR LANGUAGE AND LITERACY

Desired Result: Children are personally and socially competent.

Sample Indicators: Children show growing abilities in communication and language.

- Understands two-step requests that are sequential but not necessarily related (e.g., "Please pick up the ball and then get your coat.")

- Engages in conversations that develop a thought or an idea (e.g., tells about a past event, explains how something works)

- Plays with sounds of language in songs, rhymes, games, and stories (e.g., substitutes beginning sound of a friend's name ["Lally" for "Sally"]; claps out sounds or rhythms of language; creates own rhyming words through songs, finger plays, chanting)

- Experiments with using more complex grammar and parts of speech (e.g., uses plural forms of nouns, such as *balls* or *fishes;* uses future or past tense; or uses pronouns such as *he, she, I,* or *you*)

Desired Result: Children are effective learners.

Sample Indicator: Children demonstrate emerging literacy skills.

- Knows some letter names
- Understands that letters make up words (e.g., knows some of the letters in his or her name)
- Recognizes print in the environment (e.g., recognizes signs around the room as labels for "blocks," "drums," or "books")
- Recognizes own written name
- Makes some letter-sound correspondences
- Retells main events from a story in order

— California Department of Education, Child Development Division

Effective teachers know how to create an appropriate balance in their instructional practices between teacher-initiated and teacher-directed learning activities and child-initiated and child-directed activities. Teachers provide a variety of support, including individual and small-group work on specific skills. For example, if a child's vocabulary is limited, a teacher may arrange for more read-aloud time or more adult-mediated conversation with the child. Or the teacher may bring an interesting and unique object into the classroom to stimulate and extend language opportunities.

A balanced and comprehensive early literacy program should include these essential elements: phonological awareness, alphabet knowledge, concepts of print, vocabulary, comprehension of narrative and expository books, and emergent writing. In language development important competencies include the use of language in social contexts; the use of language to support thinking and creativity; the use of decontextualized language; and the ability to attend to the structure of a story, sentences, and words.

PHONOLOGICAL AWARENESS ACTIVITIES

Preschool teachers can use many appropriate activities to help build phonological awareness in young preschoolers and phonemic awareness in older children. Rhyming songs, syllable-clapping, and grouping objects according to how their names begin can all be used to draw children's attention to the sounds of speech. Later, to promote phonemic awareness, the activities can include:

- Isolating the first segment of a word (Let's make the first sound we hear in the word *snake*.)
- Finding all the objects on a poster that begin with the "nnn" sound
- Discovering what is left when a particular segment is removed from a word (e.g., Say *smile* without the "sss." Say *team* without the "mmm.")
- Breaking one-syllable words into their phonemes
- Blending phonemes to make a word (What word does "mmm...ooo...nnn" make?)

    — The National Research Council, *Starting Out Right: A Guide to Promoting Children's Reading Success*

Program Characteristics and Activities

- The following are examples of what children do in introductory reading activities:
  - Interact with an adult in response to hearing stories read aloud and respond to the adult's questions about the story's content.
  - Follow along as a teacher reads aloud from a Big Book and points to selected words as they are spoken.
  - Hear a book that introduces new vocabulary (for example, hear about jungle or savannah animals before visiting the zoo).
  - Play literacy-focused computer games.
  - Participate in teacher-guided discussions of read-aloud books and other shared experiences.
- The following are examples of what children do in early literacy learning activities:
  - Sing playful nursery rhymes and songs that substitute sounds in words and play with parts of words.
  - Sing entertaining alphabet songs, with accompanying print materials that allow children to see a letter simultaneously and make its sound.
  - Play rhyming games.
- The following are examples of what children do in introductory activities to writing:
  - Use writing materials in projects and pretend play.
  - Play with magnetic letters or letter blocks.
  - Engage in group games that incorporate alphabet letter names.
  - Write one's initial or name.

MAKING MY OWN BOOK

Rasheed is telling the teacher about a picture he has just drawn. "That's me, and that's my little brother," he says proudly. In large block letters the teacher writes *me* and *my brother* on two slips of paper. Then she asks Rasheed to paste the labels in the correct places on his drawing. This drawing becomes a page in a book Rasheed is creating about his life and family. Although Rasheed still does not understand the meaning of the letters and words, he is learning that letters and words do have meaning and that a sequence of pages in a book tells a story. He is learning how to tell his own story and how to think about a sequence of ideas and events. When he has enough pages in his book, he will take it home and show it to his family.

— Expert Panel, Prekindergarten Learning and Development Guidelines

2 Programs provide a language-rich and print-rich environment to support children's language and literacy learning across curricular areas.

The language and literacy learning of preschool children is greatly enhanced by an environment in which they are immersed in stimulating, useful forms of language and print. Such an environment includes the physical setup of the indoor and outdoor areas, the materials offered to children in all curricular areas, and a social and intellectual climate that supports children's creativity and pushes the limits of their language and literacy development.

Program Characteristics and Activities

- Classroom and outdoor play areas provide space for children to work and converse together comfortably during activities and projects.

- The staff is alert to opportunities to help structure and extend children's conversations and to do so unobtrusively and without dominating.

- Children are guided and supported to use their own words in a variety of social contexts to get their needs met, solve problems, and negotiate conflicts (teachers strive whenever possible not to speak for children).

- Print and print materials can be found at the children's eye level throughout the classroom and outdoor play areas.

- A specially designated reading area has a diverse, attractive selection of storybooks and nonfiction books, including appealing alphabet books.

- Relevant books, pamphlets, charts, and posters are located in such places as the art table, next to the class pet's cage, and in the mathematics area.

- Activity areas are labeled with color-coded signs, and classroom shelves are labeled with pictures and names of toys or equipment that belong in particular places.

- The writing area includes such materials as paper, pens, telephones, computer keyboards, and three-dimensional letters and numbers.

- Children are encouraged to document graphically their discoveries in mathematics, science, and art.

- Children's printed names are incorporated naturally into daily routines.

- Software packages that promote language and literacy development are available for use on the classroom computer(s).

AN EXAMPLE OF EARLY WRITING

Catherine, a confident four-year-old, was seated at the reception desk in the classroom's make-believe veterinary clinic, with the telephone receiver to her ear. As the teacher approached the desk to speak with her, Catherine continued her pretend telephone conversation and wrote furiously on a small notepad. Catherine hung up the phone and asked the teacher if she needed to see the veterinarian. "I was wondering if you have the prescription for my rabbit's medicine?" the teacher said, not wanting to interrupt the play. Smiling broadly, Catherine ripped the top sheet off the notepad and said, "I just got it from the doctor. You need to take it to the drugstore." The teacher took the prescription, noting to herself that there appeared to be a "7" among the many scribblings on the page. "I see you wrote '7' here," the teacher said, "Can you explain what that means?" Without hesitation, Catherine replied: "It means you have to give the medicine to your rabbit seven times." Asking for the prescription back, Catherine wrote two more sevens on the paper "so that you won't forget." The teacher took the prescription, thanked the beaming receptionist, and left the "office."

— Student Teacher, Mills College Children's School, Oakland, California

3 **Adults model language and literacy practices as a means to enhance children's learning and development in those areas.**

Imitation is an important means of learning among young children. When teachers or peers model language and literacy behaviors that are slightly more sophisticated than children's current levels of competence, children are appropriately challenged to develop their skills. For children to master emerging language and literacy skills, they need many opportunities to practice them. Adults provide these opportunities by listening carefully and responding thoughtfully to children when they speak, draw, or write.

Modeling of language and literacy practices is especially valuable for children who are learning to speak English. In classrooms where few children speak English as a first language, small-group activities with the teacher can be an important means to model spoken English and provide opportunities for children to develop vocabulary and concepts and to practice speaking English. Similarly, children with speech and language difficulties and children with more significant disabilities benefit from having adults or peers help interpret, model, or extend their intended communications. Regular classroom activities, such as sharing personal news during circle time, discussing favorite read-aloud stories, or dramatizing their own stories, offer children valuable practice in specific language and literacy skills over time.

Program Characteristics and Activities

- Teachers model language and literacy behaviors during conversational activities by:

    - Listening attentively to a child and checking their understanding of what the child has said

    - Engaging in meaningful conversations with children

    - Understanding and respecting the "silent periods" that may occur in children's language development

    - Responding to grammatical errors in a child's speech by modeling the correct form, not by constantly correcting the child (e.g., the child says, "Her took my toy!" and the teacher responds, "She took your toy?")

- Teachers model language and literacy behaviors during instructional activities by:

    - Reading a story aloud expressively and wondering aloud with children about what might happen next or how one of the characters might be feeling

    - Writing down a child's original story or description of an object or event

    - Listening to a child's pretend reading or encouraging attempts at writing

    - Introducing vocabulary for a discussion of specialized topics or for such subject areas as mathematics, science, or art

    - Stimulating problem solving through well-timed, open-ended questions

4 | **Programs implement a language arts curriculum that lays the foundation for children's success in language arts in elementary school.**

To establish the best conditions for all children to succeed in elementary school language arts, staff in high-quality preschool programs understand and address the link between prekindergarten language and literacy learning activities and the kindergarten curriculum. In California, language arts curricula in public schools are based on the *English–Language Arts Content Standards for California Public Schools* (California Department of Education 1998c), which outlines expected competencies at each grade level. Table 2, on the next page, illustrates some linkages between prekindergarten learning activities and the state's language arts standards for kindergarten.

Table 2

Relationship of Prekindergarten Activities and Competencies to California Language Arts Standards

Sample Prekindergarten Activities and Competencies	Selected Language Arts Standards for the End of Kindergarten	

Reading
Concepts About Print

"Read" books right-side-up and from front to back.	1.1	Identify the front cover, back cover, and title page of a book.
Begin to understand that text and illustrations convey distinct information.	1.3	Understand that printed materials provide information.

Phonemic Awareness

Listen to and recite familiar poems and chants; increase awareness and use of rhyming words and alliteration.	1.10	Identify and produce rhyming words in response to an oral prompt.
Participate in games and lessons involving separation or repetition of words and word sounds. Listen to and sing along with alphabet songs while following along in an illustrated book. Participate in activities that teach alphabet letter names.	1.12	Track auditorily each word in a sentence and each syllable in a word.
Clap in rhythms that mimic multisyllabic words and phrases.	1.13	Count the number of sounds in syllables and syllables in words.

Decoding and Word Recognition

Match, sort, and trace letters; know initial of first name; recognize some other letters.	1.14	Match all consonant and short-vowel sounds to appropriate letters.
Recognize own name (e.g., on cubby or pocket chart), names of friends; read letters in alphabet books; begin to point to highly familiar words in books.	1.15	Read simple one-syllable and high-frequency words (i.e., sight words).
Know that certain pictures (icons) go with certain labels (words); know that different icons carry different meanings.	1.16	Understand that as letters of words change, so do the sounds (i.e., the alphabetic principle).

Note: Detailed descriptions of and rationales for early language and literacy learning activities are included in *First Class: A Guide for Early Primary Education* (California Department of Education 1999b).

Table 2 (Continued)

Relationship of Prekindergarten Activities and Competencies to California Language Arts Standards

Sample Prekindergarten Activities and Competencies	Selected Language Arts Standards for the End of Kindergarten
Vocabulary and Concept Development	
Have many opportunities to converse with adults and peers about a variety of people, objects, activities, events, and ideas in the environment; sort objects by category.	1.17 Identify and sort common words in basic categories (e.g., colors, shapes, foods).
Identify common objects in the environment. Regularly learn new vocabulary through activities, conversation, and teacher-guided instruction.	1.18 Describe common objects and events in both general and specific language.
Reading Comprehension	
Offer plausible predictions about a story during the initial reading; predict the next events in a story after several readings; plan and carry out a sequence of actions in the classroom.	2.2 Use pictures and context to make predictions about story content.
Contribute relevant personal experiences and prior knowledge during storybook reading; tell (oral) stories about self and family; respond to teacher requests to relate personal knowledge and experience to text.	2.3 Connect to life experiences the information and events in texts.
Literary Response and Analysis	
Have many opportunities to hear interesting, culturally diverse stories read aloud; attend to storybook reading or storybook tapes; respond orally during storybook reading; draw pictures based on a story and talk about drawing; act out stories; spontaneously discuss stories.	3.3 Identify characters, settings, and important events.
Writing Strategies	
Draw pictures to represent people, objects, events, or concepts (e.g. winter); make controlled and uncontrolled scribbles and name the scribbles or describe their meaning; make mock letters, letter strings, letter groups; label pictures; write initial or whole name.	1.1 Use letters and phonetically spelled words to write about experiences, stories, people, objects, or events.
Listening and Speaking	
Have many and varied opportunities in a supportive, stimulating environment to converse with adults and peers about topics of personal interest and importance and about topics beyond direct, current experience.	1.2 Share information and ideas, speaking audibly in complete, coherent sentences.

Program Characteristics and Activities

■ Teachers have knowledge of the continuum of children's language and literacy development and its relationship to the language arts competencies expected of children in kindergarten and the early primary grades.

■ Teachers understand their role in facilitating early language and literacy learning.

■ Teachers conduct ongoing and varied assessments of each child's language and early literacy development to provide needed learning experiences.

■ Teachers conduct individual, small-group, and large-group activities that address specific language and literacy learning goals (e.g., expressive language or alphabet letter names).

5 The program recognizes and includes the home languages of English learners.

Language development is important for a child's general cognitive development. By the age of three, children have developed many cognitive skills using their first, or "home," language. Research evidence suggests that development of a first language serves as a foundation for acquisition of a second language (Garcia and others 1995). Because of different learning styles, personalities, and levels of motivation, English learners will use different strategies and progress at varying rates. Effective preschool teachers are patient and consistent in helping those children.

Program Characteristics and Activities

■ The program staff understands the general process of learning a second language and knows that there are individual differences in each child's rate and method of learning a second language. For example, a child may process simple interactions in English but process more complex interactions or activities in the home language, increasing the processing time in some situations.

■ High-quality programs include basic information for parents on how children acquire a first and a second language.

■ Adults support acquisition of a first and a second language by listening carefully, following the child's lead in conversation, expanding on what the child says, and showing interest and attentiveness during conversation with the child.

■ Adults proficient in an English learner's home language maintain a link between the school and home.

■ Preschool teachers who do not speak the child's home language work with parents and other staff members who do.

- The staff uses families as resources to understand a bilingual child's proficiency in both the home language and English.

- English learners have opportunities to hear and use their home language in the course of daily classroom activities.

- All children have opportunities to learn words from other children's home languages.

LANGUAGE-RICH ENVIRONMENTS

In addition to maintaining an awareness of cultural differences, preschool teachers need to provide all children with language-rich environments. A number of strategies enrich language in the child's environment. At the language-acquisition preschool at the University of Kansas, strategies have been developed to foster language development in . . . language-impaired children and [English learners] (Rice 1991). The strategies identified in this program are:

1. Provide opportunities for language use and interaction.

   • Provide rich, interesting activities worth talking about.

   • Allow times when teachers are not talking and children can initiate conversation.

   • Arrange the environment so that some materials are inaccessible—as a method to promote discussion.

2. Provide focused stimulation on particular language features.

   • Model target sounds or words for children; encourage (but do not require) repetition of models.

   • Recast children's utterances to maintain the meaning but use a slightly more grammatically complex way of speaking.

   • Recast adult utterances in the same way.

3. Develop routines to help children connect events and language.

   • Establish familiar daily routines, such as an arrival time, circle time, and snack time.

   • Develop scripts related to dramatic play activities, including discussion/demonstration about roles, props, and activities.

   • Use event casting ("talking while doing") to model problem-solving strategies.

4. Stimulate social interactions between children.

   • Redirect children's requests to other children; provide a model if necessary.

All of these strategies are based on the assumption that language is acquired in social settings in which children construct their language from the speech of adults and more capable peers.

— California Department of Education, *Fostering the Development of a First and a Second Language in Early Childhood: Resource Guide*

BILINGUAL ADULTS IN THE CLASSROOM

Bilingual adults—teachers, paraprofessionals, or parents—can be especially helpful in supporting English learners either in English or in the students' primary language. By helping children understand what is expected of them, bilingual adults promote children's access to the curriculum. They increase children's opportunities to engage in more complex language and thinking by enabling children to use their primary language in classroom settings at the same time as they are learning English. They help to ensure that assessment is accurate and reflects children's actual competence levels. They also demonstrate to children that their language and the culture it expresses are valued in the classroom.

— K. Au, "Social Constructivism and the School: Literacy of Students of Diverse Backgrounds," *Journal of Literacy Research*

6 | **Children's language and literacy development is supported through interaction between the preschool staff and the children's families.**

Development of language and literacy skills benefits from a close working partnership between the home and school (Bus, van IJzendoorn, and Pellegrini 1995; Whitehurst and Lonigan 1998). Dialogue between the school and home requires special effort and sensitivity when the social and cultural backgrounds of teachers and families differ. A child's home language and literacy practices are central to the child's personal and cultural identity. Teachers may need to initiate a discussion with the family to discover a child's language and literacy interests and abilities, especially if a child speaks a different language at home from that spoken at school.

Program Characteristics and Activities

- During social and instructional conversations at preschool, children are encouraged to talk about their families and homes as a way to reinforce the link between home and school. Teachers are careful, however, about the need to respect families' confidentiality and privacy.

- Teachers offer to send print and other materials (for example, books, audiotapes, videotapes, or board games) home to support the child's language and literacy learning in the family.

- Children's literature, translated into families' primary languages, is available.

- Older children are invited to provide support for primary-language retellings, dramatizations, and puppet shows.

- Teachers encourage the use of oral traditions found in some language groups as a way to engage parents in their children's learning of English, even when they do not speak or read English. For example, teachers might invite parents to observe their child engaged in storybook "reading" and then encourage the parents to use the story's illustrations to retell the story at home, either in English or in the home language.

DEVELOPING PHONOLOGICAL AWARENESS

Phonological awareness plays a crucial role in learning to read. The development of this ability typically begins by about age three and improves gradually over time. Because the early success in this skill is predictive of future reading achievement, researchers have begun to investigate the possibility of enhancing the development of phonological awareness prior to the start of school.

It is clear that to increase school preparedness of children at risk of future reading difficulties due to economic disadvantage and other factors, instruction in phonological awareness should be accompanied by training in letters and letter-sound associations. Children who enter school with these competencies will be better prepared to benefit from formal reading instruction.

— Adapted from National Research Council, *Preventing Reading Difficulties in Young Children*

Mathematics Learning and Development

Mathematics is a way of thinking about the world and observing and describing it in numbers, shapes, patterns, and general rules. During the past two decades, much has been learned about the development of mathematical thinking in young children. Child development researchers have found that mathematical knowledge begins during infancy and undergoes extensive development during the first five years of life. It is just as natural for young children to think mathematically as it is for them to use language (Geary 1994).

Nevertheless, young children's mathematical thinking is informal—that is, it involves the manipulation of concrete objects and sets of objects. The informal mathematical thinking of young children serves as a foundation for the development of formal mathematical thinking in elementary school children. Formal mathematical thinking is a more abstract endeavor involving mathematical notations, such as the written numerals and operation signs as in 2 + 2 = 4.

THE JOY OF MATHEMATICS

Good early mathematics is broader and deeper than early practice of "school skills." Quality mathematics is a joy, not a pressure. It is the sum of the experiences children have from birth related to number, space, and patterns. It includes the parent placing cereal in a toddler's hands, saying, "Here are two pieces. One, two!" It includes drawing a "treasure map" of the backyard. It includes noticing that two chants for skipping rope have the same pattern.

— D. H. Clements, "Playing Math with Young Children," *Curriculum Administrator*

Mathematical Development from Birth to Age Three

Mathematical knowledge emerges surprisingly early—during infancy—and it develops considerably during the first three years of life. By twenty-four months of age, many toddlers have learned their first number word (typically *two*) and sometimes use *two* in the presence of a set of two objects (Wagner and Walters 1982). The words *one* and *three* are usually acquired and used appropriately within the next twelve months. Depending on the early environment, children begin to try to count using verbal number names at age two or three years, and counting continues to develop and improve with age and practice throughout the preschool years (Gelman and Gallistel 1978; Wynn 1990). During the first three years of life, infants and toddlers have already begun to acquire knowledge about number and space and are especially proficient with small, concrete sets.

Mathematical Development from Ages Three Through Five

Children's informal mathematical knowledge develops rapidly during the preschool years. Several important developments can be identified during this period, but their timing varies considerably from one child to the next, often by as much as a year. This variation is due, at least in part, to variations in children's home and preschool learning environments (Ginsburg and Russell 1981; Saxe, Guberman, and Gearhart 1987; Starkey and Klein 1992).

Counting and one-to-one correspondence. Important developments in counting and understanding of one-to-one correspondence occur during the preschool years. Counting becomes well-grounded conceptually in three-year-olds. The easiest type of set for three-year-olds to count contains only a few objects, is arranged in a straight line, and can be touched as children proceed with their counting. From three through five years of age, children acquire skills as they practice counting, and they become able to cope with numerically larger sets in different arrangements without needing to touch or move objects while counting (Greeno, Riley, and Gelman 1984). Children also learn more about number words *(one, two, three)* because they have a desire to count larger sets and a curiosity about the number word system itself (Fuson 1988).

Children's understanding and use of one-to-one correspondence also advance during this period of development. Many three-year-olds judge that two sets are equal if the objects in one set are placed in spatial one-to-one correspondence (e.g., next to) with the objects in another set. By age four many children use one-to-one correspondence to create a set equal to one that has already been constructed (Piaget and Szeminska 1952).

Knowledge of arithmetic. Children from three through five years of age undergo a marked change in their knowledge of arithmetic. Three-year-olds can mentally calculate sums and remainders produced when small sets of objects increase or decrease in number. They usually make mistakes with larger sets, however, often guessing the sum or remainder. Many four- and five-year-olds overcome this set-size limitation by inventing strategies for calculating larger sums and remainders (Siegler and Robinson 1982). Children's strategies typically involve counting or holding up fingers to represent a set of objects that is being calculated.

When children are about three years of age, their knowledge of simple division also emerges. For example, preschoolers become able to share or distribute a set of objects equally between two toy animals (Klein and Langer 1991). Three-year-olds can divide a visible set into equal subsets (quotients) if the subsets are very small, but they cannot do so consistently if subsets are larger.

Quantity and measurement. Another type of mathematical knowledge that children develop during the preschool years is an understanding of quantity and measurement. Preschool children know that such properties as mass (amount), length, and weight exist, but they do not initially know how to reason about these properties or how to measure them accurately. If three-year-olds have some quantity of a substance (e.g., clay) and then are given an additional amount (more clay), they know that they have more than they did before. Three- and four-year-olds encounter difficulty, however, when asked to judge which of two quantities that they currently have (e.g., which of two mounds of clay) is more (Piaget 1970). Three- and four-year-olds lack basic measurement rules, such as lining up an end when comparing the lengths of two objects. However, many children, at ages four to five with training, can become less dependent on perceptual cues and thus make progress in reasoning about or measuring quantities (Gelman 1982; Starkey and Klein 2000).

Spatial and geometric knowledge. Children's spatial and geometric knowledge also develops rapidly during the preschool years. Children make progress in naming and creating common two- and three-dimensional shapes. Older preschoolers become able to analyze the properties of shapes, such as the number of sides of a triangle (Clements and Battista 1992), and to compare corresponding geometric shapes that have undergone a transformation, such as rotation or flip (Beilin and Klein 1982).

ALL TEACHERS CAN TEACH MATHEMATICS

All preschool teachers are teachers of mathematics who can have a powerful impact on children's mathematical thinking and later achievement and success in elementary school and beyond. Teachers, however, may not realize the extent to which current classroom activities and their own practices support mathematics. Ideally, teachers will experience the kinds of professional development that instills understanding and enthusiasm for mathematics, a degree of pleasure and comfort in teaching mathematics, and an appreciation of the many ways in which mathematics is linked to children's creativity and development of analytical, problem-solving, and logical-thinking skills.

— Expert Panel, Prekindergarten Learning and Development Guidelines

Research has revealed much about the nature and development of mathematical thinking in young children. Although children's informal mathematical knowledge clearly emerges during the first five years of life, environmental support is necessary to develop a broad foundation of informal mathematical knowledge before children enter kindergarten. Wide variations in the degree of support children receive for mathematical development, however, produce large differences in children's knowledge of informal mathematics (Ginsburg, Klein, and Starkey 1998; Starkey and Klein 2000). These disparities make it especially important to provide all children with a broad base of support for mathematics at home and in preschool.

Informal Mathematics Knowledge as a Foundation

The informal mathematical knowledge of the preschool child described previously serves as a foundation for the acquisition of formal mathematical knowledge in elementary school. Table 3, "Relationship of Young Children's Informal Mathematical Knowledge to the Mathematics Content Standards," illustrates the articulation of informal mathematics knowledge with the *Mathematics Content Standards for California Public Schools* (California Department of Education 1999d).

Table 3

Relationship of Young Children's Informal Mathematical Knowledge to the Mathematics Content Standards	
Sample Prekindergarten Activities and Competencies	**Strand from the Kindergarten Mathematics Content Standards**

Children can do the following:
 	
• Count to ten.
• Understand that number represents quantity (e.g., can get three apples out of a box).
• Enumerate small sets by subitizing (nonverbal counting of sets of four or fewer).
• Use and manipulate concrete objects.
• Practice one-to-one correspondence.
• Match sets.
• Practice addition, subtraction, and division by using manipulatives and other concrete objects (e.g., distributing a snack equitably; folding a paper into two equal parts).
• Make comparisons of a relative quantity.
• Recognize attribute variance (e.g., color, shape, size).
	Number Sense
	
	1.0 Students understand the relationship between numbers and quantities (i.e., that a set of objects has the same number of objects in different situations regardless of its position or arrangement):
	
	   1.1 Compare two or more sets of objects (up to ten objects in each group) and identify which set is equal to, more than, or less than the other.
	
	   1.2 Count, recognize, represent, name, and order a number of objects (up to 30).
	
	   1.3 Know that the larger numbers describe sets with more objects in them than the smaller numbers have.
	
	2.0 Students understand and describe simple additions and subtractions.
	
	   2.1 Use concrete objects to determine the answers to addition and subtraction problems (for two numbers that are each less than 10).

Children can do the following: • Classify objects according to one characteristic (e.g. blue bears, red bears, or yellow bears). • Begin to classify by multiple characteristics (e.g., from a group of mixed color and size of bears, sorts big blue bears and small blue bears).	**Algebra and Functions** 1.0 Students sort and classify objects: 1.1 Identify, sort, and classify objects by attribute and identify objects that do not belong to a particular group (e.g., all these balls are green, those are red).

Table 3 (Continued)

Relationship of Young Children's Informal Mathematical Knowledge to the Mathematics Content Standards

Sample Prekindergarten Activities and Competencies	Strand from the Kindergarten Mathematics Content Standards
Children can do the following: • Make direct comparison of quantities (e.g., length or weight of objects). • Use nonstandard measurement (e.g., creation of a nonstandard unit to determine relative length or weight). • Demonstrate knowledge of shapes (identify, describe, and compare properties of specific two- and three-dimensional shapes; recognize a circle, square, and triangle). • Demonstrate knowledge of relative spatial position in two-dimensional grids (e.g., above/below, left/right). • Arrange objects from smallest to largest (e.g., nesting cups, graduated blocks). • Understand ordinal concepts: *before, after, what comes next, yesterday,* and *tomorrow.*	**Measurement and Geometry** 1.0 Students understand the concept of time and units to measure it; they understand that objects have properties, such as length, weight, and capacity, and that comparisons may be made by referring to those properties: 　1.1 Compare the length, weight, and capacity of objects by making direct comparisons with reference objects (e.g., note which object is shorter, longer, taller, lighter, heavier, or holds more). 　1.2 Demonstrate an understanding of concepts of time (e.g., morning, afternoon, evening, today, yesterday, tomorrow, week, year) and tools that measure time (e.g., clock, calendar). 2.0 Students identify common objects in their environment and describe the geometric features: 　2.1 Identify and describe common geometric objects (e.g., circle, triangle, square, rectangle, cube, sphere, cone).
Children can do the following: • Demonstrate pattern knowledge (match objects to established pattern, identify and describe patterns; distinguish patterns from nonpatterns; use rhythm and repetition). • Participate with teacher in the use of graphs and charts to represent and organize information. • Understand abstract concepts of *some, all, none.*	**Statistics, Data Analysis, and Probability** 1.0 Students collect information about objects and events in their environment: 　1.1 Identify, describe, and extend simple patterns (such as circles or triangles) by referring to their shapes, sizes, or colors.
Children can do the following: • Employ reasoning strategies using number and geometric shapes (e.g., use objects or finger counting in addition, subtraction; construct objects using unit blocks). • Can function in their environment (e.g., able to move and experience themselves in space).	**Mathematical Reasoning** 2.0 Students solve problems in reasonable ways and justify their reasoning.

GUIDELINES

1	**The program develops and builds on children's existing informal mathematical knowledge, recognizing that children enter preschool with different experiences in mathematics.**

When children begin preschool, an effective program recognizes and assesses each child's knowledge, developmental levels, and skills. It continues to develop children's mathematical knowledge, and it begins the process of connecting this informal knowledge to formal knowledge, which relies more specifically on mathematical symbols (numbers, operational notations) and abstractions.

Program Characteristics and Activities

- Activities are designed to accommodate individual children's different levels of mathematical development. For example, an activity designed to identify shapes may include models of simple two-dimensional shapes, such as a square and triangle, and more complex two-dimensional shapes, such as a hexagon, an octagon, and a rhombus.

- As kindergarten approaches, the teacher provides opportunities for older children to hear and use mathematical language and numbers. To be meaningful, the process should incorporate the use of manipulatives.

2	**Teacher-guided and child-initiated activities are integrated in a mathematically rich learning environment, using multiple instructional approaches.**

Teacher-guided activities ensure that all children's mathematical development is supported and enriched. These activities are particularly important for children who come to school with relatively little knowledge of mathematics. An effective program includes a balance of teacher-guided and child-initiated activities. The program provides a rich environment for mathematical learning, with a wide variety of opportunities and materials for children to use in mathematical thinking. Teachers are continually aware of mathematical "teachable moments" and windows of opportunity in all subjects throughout the day, not just during "math time."

To ensure that all children advance in their knowledge of mathematics, staff members in effective preschool programs provide a wide variety of mathematical learning opportunities that match children's diverse learning styles and abilities. There are mathematical situations and problems for all children to solve in different places and different ways every day. Combinations of these opportunities in structured and unstructured and individual and group settings enrich mathematics learning and increase each child's exposure to mathematics concepts.

The teacher uses many contexts and approaches to develop mathematical vocabulary and concepts, creating and facilitating situations in which children can learn about mathematics through play, structured individual activities, and small-group sessions.

Program Characteristics and Activities

- Opportunities to learn mathematics abound throughout the preschool environment.

- Materials are regularly changed and replenished in a designated mathematics area.

- Math-related posters, word labels, graphs, and countable objects can be found throughout the room.

- Children have opportunities to engage in mathematics in every area of the program environment because it is integrated into other curricular subjects. For example, countable objects are located in many places other than the mathematics center. There may be money to count in a play store area, numbers to identify on a telephone in the housekeeping area, shape molds in the sand table, and measuring cups in the water table.

- A computer with appropriate mathematics software may also be available.

MATHEMATICAL THINKING IN EVERYDAY ACTIVITIES

- Informal measuring (e.g., creating matching piles of sand in the sand box)
- Singing songs, such as "Five Little Ducks Went Out One Day," incorporating finger play with counting
- Completing picture puzzles with pieces of different sizes and shapes
- Comparing the properties of objects or the sequence of events using such mathematical terms as *bigger, smaller, shorter, taller, heavier, lighter, less, more, sooner, later, before, after, nearer,* and *farther*
- Playing with and identifying by name blocks of different shapes (e.g., squares, rectangles, triangles, and circles)
- Identifying objects in the shape of squares, rectangles, triangles, and circles in the classroom or center and outdoors while on walks

MATHEMATICAL THINKING IN SOCIAL SITUATIONS

Teachers should observe children at play or during snack time and focus on their use of mathematical language in situations where mathematics is used. The following activities can be used to expand mathematics learning:

- Distribute dishes in playhouse (division).
- Sort toys to use or share (logical reasoning).
- Put away unit blocks, matching the shapes (spatial sense).
- Pour sand and fill containers (measurement).
- Count cups, napkins, and crackers (number sense).
- Observe and describe patterns on clothing (pattern identification).

The teacher may occasionally intervene in such play to ask questions that help children solve a problem or focus their interest. "Math talk" in social conversation or in a game-like atmosphere can increase mathematical thinking. Examples of "math talk" may include the following activities:

- Discuss how many crackers each child should take from the basket; count how many children are at the table; count the number of empty chairs.
- Discuss how many children came to school today or how many are missing from the group.

— Adapted from W. H. Dutton, A. Dutton, and B. Dutton, *Mathematics Children Use and Understand*

LEARNING MATHEMATICS THROUGH PLAY

- When cleaning up the room, ask the children to put things into two piles that belong together. Almost any group of things in the program setting can be sorted in some way. Sort things one way, and next time sort them another way. Let the children use their imagination to come up with different sorting rules.

- Four- and five-year-olds love to play with puzzles and board games. These activities help children learn mathematics concepts, such as counting, planning ahead, thinking of and finding patterns, and understanding quantities. When you play with the children, share your successful strategies for playing with them.

- Children enjoy building together in the block corner. Because blocks have three-dimensional shapes and can be handled, children can use them to combine and change shapes. They learn to recognize geometry in the real world and the relationships between and among shapes. By fitting one shape over another—for example, a pyramid over a cube to make a house figure—they can see how the shapes relate to each other. When children build with blocks, make sure to ask them why they are using certain shapes. This question makes them think about what they are doing.

- Ask the children to estimate who among them is the tallest and then let them figure out how to do the measuring. This simple activity will help them develop a sound understanding of number sense, measurement, and estimation.

- Give the children old cardboard boxes to climb in and out of. You can even open the two ends to make a tunnel for them to crawl through. This is an enjoyable activity, and children have the opportunity to experience themselves in space.

- Children can learn about numbers and counting by playing many different games with dice and dominoes. They will practice counting and learn which numbers are bigger and smaller than others, and after a while they will begin to know how many dots are on each cube just by seeing them and without counting them each time.

— Adapted from C. S. Fromboluti and N. Rinck, *Early Childhood: Where Learning Begins—Mathematics*

---

3 | **The program implements a mathematics curriculum that lays the foundation for children's success in mathematics in elementary school.**

All children come to preschool with some degree of informal mathematical ability. The purpose of a strong preschool mathematics program should be to enhance and strengthen children's informal mathematical abilities and to build a firm foundation for the more formal learning that begins in kindergarten.

Program Characteristics and Activities

- Teachers consider both children's current level of mathematical knowledge and ways to enrich the knowledge and skills of children as they move toward kindergarten.

- Teachers are knowledgeable about the standards and emphasize meaningful and age-appropriate activities.

- Teachers design mathematics activities to provide experience and practice of concepts included in the *Mathematics Content Standards* (e.g., number sense, measurement, and geometry).

MATHEMATICS GAMES FOR TWO OR MORE CHILDREN

- Set up a mystery game in which children can feel shapes hidden inside a paper bag and then identify them. Ask each child one at a time to reach in and feel the shape inside the bag. Set up five shapes on the table that match the shapes in the bag. Ask each child to match the shape on the table with the shape in the bag.

- Set out on a table various small objects with holes. Children love to string different types of small objects with large holes to make necklaces and other jewelry. This activity helps them practice sorting and making simple patterns.

- Have a treasure hunt. Give each child a paper bag and ask the children to find things of a particular shape that you have put around the room or outside.

    — Adapted from C. S. Fromboluti and N. Rinck, *Early Childhood: Where Learning Begins—Mathematics*

DESIRED RESULTS FOR MATHEMATICS

Desired Result: Children are effective learners.

Sample Indicators: Children show interest in real-life mathematical concepts.

- Recognizes squares, circles, and triangles (e.g., names "circle" and matches it to other circles in the room)

- Describes how items are the same or different (e.g., "This ball is bigger than that one." "My shirt is the same as Marcus's.")

- Matches and names simple patterns (e.g., "boy-girl, boy-girl," "red-blue, red-blue")

- Locates things in a familiar environment (e.g., finds the block corner; knows that the bathroom is around the corner down the hall; can clean up the dramatic play area in an organized way)

- Estimates (e.g., "I'm as tall as the yellow bookshelf.")

    — California Department of Education, Child Development Division

4 | The program identifies clear, age-appropriate goals for mathematics learning and development.

Goals for mathematics learning and development should be clearly stated, age-appropriate, and continually monitored and revised as necessary. As much as possible, the teacher and all program staff should be aware of ways throughout the day to help all children develop their mathematical thinking based on what they already know and are able to do.

Program Characteristics and Activities

- A clearly stated set of goals for mathematics learning and development is shared with program staff and parents.

- The teacher and other staff regularly monitor implementation of the mathematics program and refine it as necessary to meet the stated goals.

- The children's mathematical learning and development are regularly assessed to determine how well they are achieving the program's goals for mathematics.

ADDING AND SUBTRACTING WITH CONCRETE OBJECTS: THE GOLDFISH GAME

Developmental Prerequisites: This activity is appropriate for preschool children who can count a small set of objects (e.g., one to five objects) and can construct a small set of objects when given a verbal number name (e.g., "five").

The goals of this small-group activity are to teach children how to act out addition and subtraction operations with concrete objects (small cardboard or plastic goldfish) in the context of a story and to count the sets of objects after each operation in the story to determine the result.

At the beginning of the activity, the teacher gives each child a story mat that is half blue and half green, a cup attached to the story mat, and a set of seven goldfish in the cup. The teacher introduces the activity by saying, "We are going to hear a story about a whale who loves to eat little goldfish." Each child will play the part of the whale and will get to eat goldfish. Then the teacher reminds the children to listen carefully to find out what to do. The teacher tells the following story:

> Five fish swim into the ocean. (Each child puts five goldfish into the blue half of the story mat.) Two fish swim too close to the whale, and he gobbles up two of the fish. (Child subtracts/eats two goldfish from the story mat.) How many fish are left in the ocean? (Child counts the remaining goldfish and states the number three.) The whale is still hungry, so he swims over and gobbles up two more fish. (Child subtracts/eats two more goldfish from the story mat.) How many fish are left in the ocean? (Child counts the remaining goldfish or states the number one.) Now two more fish swim into the ocean to join their friend. (Each child adds/puts two more goldfish onto the story mat.) How many fish are in the ocean altogether? (Child counts all the goldfish on the story mat and states the number three.)

The teacher helps the children as needed throughout the activity and collects all the extra goldfish before playing the game again.

— Adapted from A. Klein and P. Starkey, *Berkeley Math Readiness Curriculum*

5 The program establishes a partnership with parents and other caregivers in preparing children for mathematics learning.

The preschool mathematics program should be supported and understood at home. To gain this support, the teacher needs to communicate with parents and other caregivers about age-appropriate expectations for mathematics learning at the preschool level. The teacher also needs to establish continuing communication with each family about the child's progress and ways to support mathematical learning. For example, there may be a need to inform parents that being able to count to high numbers does not necessarily mean that young children have an understanding of concepts essential to further progress in mathematics.

Program Characteristics and Activities

- The program provides parents with family education classes, letters, newsletters, and other materials to help their children with preschool mathematics.

- The program offers parents information about the mathematics curriculum and encourages parents to talk to their children about mathematical ideas and to share information with each other and with their child's teacher about how they are supporting mathematics at home.

- Throughout the program year the staff provides parents with information about their child's mathematical development and progress.

Physical and Motor Development

The preschooler is often a bundle of energy who never walks when running is an option and who sees every puddle as an invitation to jump. Well-designed preschool programs and environments take advantage of this natural energy by providing a wide range of opportunities for children to develop physically, to stay strong and healthy, and to refine a variety of physical skills. For children who have limited access to appropriate outdoor play areas, the preschool may be one setting in the child's day that offers a variety of opportunities for healthy physical development.

Well-designed programs accommodate a wide range of developmental rates and physical abilities. Most of the literature on children's physical well-being and motor development focuses on developmental milestones, specific behaviors, and capabilities that indicate whether a child's growth is "on target" with normal development. Equally important is a more inclusive definition that encompasses the wide range of children's physical capabilities.

All children are entitled to develop physically in a well-designed early care and education program, including children with physical or developmental problems. Children with health problems should receive extra consideration; their absenteeism may be due to illness or medical appointments. Teachers should reach out to children who have such problems and engage them in the program routine and activities to prevent social isolation and promote greater interaction with others. Inclusion of children with special needs or disabilities, in addition to being required by law, is beneficial to all the children in the program and promotes greater understanding and acceptance of others.

DESIRED RESULTS FOR PHYSICAL AND MOTOR COMPETENCE

Desired Result: Children show physical and motor competence.

Sample Indicators: Children demonstrate an increased proficiency in motor skills.

Gross motor skills: *Ability to maintain stability in various positions (balance) and to move from one position to another (positional change):*

- Shows greater balance and control
- Speeds up and slows down
- Runs and stops quickly
- Avoids obstacles (e.g., moves about the room without bumping into objects)
- Climbs stairs without holding onto the railing
- Pedals a tricycle
- Kicks a large ball

Fine motor skills: *Eye-hand, or skilled sensory, coordination to implement goal-directed fine motor movements:*

- Shows increasing eye-hand coordination, strength, and control to perform fine motor skills
- Manipulates two small objects at the same time (e.g., stringing beads)
- Uses tools with increasing precision (e.g., hammer, hole punch, scissors)
- Zips zippers
- Fastens buttons

— California Department of Education, Child Development Division

MOTOR SKILL DEVELOPMENT

Children are physical beings. Anyone entering a preschool classroom cannot help but be aware of children's constant activity and movement. We know that children's physical and motor development influences, and is influenced by, all other aspects of development: cognitive, language, social, and emotional. Even so, early childhood teachers too often believe that a child's motor skills will develop on their own. Therefore, they do not consciously plan for motor skill development as they do for other areas.

> — C. Benelli and B. Youngue, "Supporting Young Children's Motor Skill Development," *Childhood Education*

GUIDELINES

1 | **The curriculum gives attention to all areas of motor skill development, including gross motor, fine motor, oral motor, and sensorimotor.**

Well-designed early care and education programs encourage children to develop all their physical skills and abilities through a variety of activities. Children often have a preference for a particular skill and will naturally focus on areas in which they feel the most comfortable. For example, the boy who loves to make detailed clay figures may be reluctant to try his hand at walking a balance beam. A girl who can do expert cartwheels may need help in fine motor activities, such as cutting with scissors. Every child should be encouraged to test his or her physical limitations without ridicule or fear of failure.

Program Characteristics and Activities

- Programs promote skill development and time to practice the following:
  - Gross motor skills: running, jumping, climbing, skipping, and dancing
  - Fine motor skills: cutting, painting, threading, pouring, molding, buttoning, zipping, tying, and doing finger play
  - Sensorimotor skills: catching, pointing, matching, touching, and clapping
  - Oral motor skills: talking, singing, imitating sounds, rhyming, and chanting

MIRROR GAME

Children pair off and stand facing each other. One partner performs a series of simple movements (standing in place), which the second partner imitates. After a while the partners reverse roles. The object is not to try to trick each other but to produce a mirror reflection as closely as possible.

This cooperative activity, while providing practice with nonlocomotor movement, helps broaden children's movement vocabularies by exposing them to the movements of someone else. Additionally, the movement element of shape is explored, and children are given an opportunity to physically replicate what their eyes are seeing—both important concepts in art, and the latter a necessary skill in language arts.

— R. Pica, "Beyond Physical Development: Why Young Children Need to Move," *Young Children*

4 Teachers consider children's special health and physical needs when designing physical activities.

All activities should be adapted to allow full participation by all children, but when this accommodation is not possible, special activities may need to be developed. Under those circumstances, children with special needs should be paired with nondisabled children. This arrangement will decrease the feeling of isolation experienced by children with special needs and allow nondisabled children to develop friendships with and an understanding of those children.

Program Characteristics and Activities

- If a child cannot run, the teacher occasionally practices slow-motion movement with the class.

- If a child has special nutritional needs, the teacher helps the child to accept that his or her lunch or snack differs from that of the group. The teacher may invite the parents to prepare samples for the whole class to taste.

- Teachers keep medications to be administered during program hours locked and out of children's reach.

- Teachers adapt equipment so that all children can play.

- Teachers help children, if necessary, in using and playing with toys and equipment.

- Teachers adapt activities, make accommodations, and modify strategies to integrate children socially and enable them to participate in activities.

Other Curriculum Content Areas

High-quality preschool curriculum is a rich, seamlessly integrated collection of program routines, learning activities, free play, and projects, each encompassing many domains of development. This wealth of activities encourages each child to choose activities and participate on the basis of his or her interests, skills, and preferred learning styles. Four essential curricular areas not addressed in detail in this document contribute significantly to a rich preschool curriculum: social studies, science, creative arts (visual arts, music, drama, dance), and health and nutrition.

Opportunities for Investigation

The other content areas offer children specific ways to investigate the world and to communicate their discoveries to others. For example, many young children are drawn to exploring the various structures, roles, and traditions of families, a key focus of preschool social studies. Typically, this exploration takes place in the context of one-on-one or small-group conversations or during imaginary play.

Skilled preschool teachers are alert to such spontaneous activities as a source of ideas for a more focused activity; for example, read-aloud stories about diverse families, program visits by infant siblings, or cooking projects involving favorite family foods. Science, creative arts, and health offer equally important and varied opportunities to support children's acquisition of knowledge and skills. One overarching guideline encompasses all four content areas.

GUIDELINE

1

The teacher builds on the natural curiosity that children have about the world around them by creating opportunities for exploration of social studies, science, the arts, and health and nutrition. These subjects are part of the program's daily routines and are fully integrated into the program.

Where appropriate, the program links these content areas with other content areas, such as social–emotional development, language and literacy development, mathematics, and physical and motor development.

Young children come to preschool with an instinctive desire to explore the world; this interest should be continually encouraged. Although what most young children know about the world is tied to their personal experience, the preschool should be rich with materials and interesting starting points for exploration. Costumes for dramatic play, indoor and outdoor gardens, small animals, snack time, stories, songs, games, occasional field trips—all are potential starting points for discovery and learning.

As much as possible, children should have a variety of opportunities to develop their individual interests and potential. Exploring a variety of content areas is one way to accept and encourage the success of diverse groups of children. All children will find ways to excel when many different learning opportunities are available, and children are encouraged to become engaged in activities that genuinely interest them.

Learning opportunities for children flow as easily from music and the arts as they do from health, safety, or nutrition. Music and the arts are universal languages that can encourage many kinds of communication that complement and enhance the program's emphasis on language and literacy. To develop children's awareness of health, safety, or nutrition, the teacher takes time regularly to discuss appropriate health habits and practices outside the program, such as preventive medical checkups (i.e., going to the doctor), traffic safety, or eating nutritious foods.

An especially useful and interesting approach to integrating different content areas is through projects. A successful project begins with a topic that is interesting to children; for example, animals in the zoo, plants in the garden, the post office, or the auto mechanics shop down the street from the early care and education center. Building on this interest, teachers can answer questions firsthand in a natural way as children draw, make models, tell stories, and explore questions about the topic. The teacher's role throughout the project is to facilitate and stimulate the exploration.

THE PROJECT APPROACH

A project is an extended, in-depth investigation of a topic, ideally one worthy of the children's attention and energy. In other words projects involve children in conducting research on phenomena and events worth learning about in their own environments.

In the process of these investigations, children have opportunities to pose questions, to generate theories and predictions concerning possible answers, to seek answers to their questions (answers from which they are likely to generate still more questions), to interview experts and others from whom relevant information can be obtained, and to engage in other activities involved in collecting information.

Projects provide contexts in which children can apply a wide variety of social and intellectual skills, in addition to the basic academic skills being learned in the more formal parts of the curriculum.

— ERIC/EECE, *The Project Approach Catalog*

THE RAIN FOREST PROJECT

A classroom parent who was working as a physician in the jungles of Central America sent photographs and letters to the children. After seeing the photos and hearing about the jungles, several children decided that a climbing loft structure in the room could be a rain forest. Now the loft is decorated with large paper leaves and trailing vines painted in bright greens and yellows. Posted on nearby walls are photographs and short descriptions dictated by the children documenting how they built their rain forest.

One day in our classroom Max declared our loft a rain forest. He moved several potted plants into the space and began to enact his interpretation of a rain forest monkey. This activity attracted many other children who joined Max, each playing out his or her own animal character in the rain forest. For many days this play continued, spilling out into many other aspects of school life. In the atelier [creative arts studio], children face-painted themselves to look like the animals they wanted to become and developed inclusive play themes that allowed for further expression of their animalness out in the yard. The animals also appeared in plays, drawings, and discussions as the children explored the varied aspects of rain forest life. The children expressed interest in and concern about the rain forest environment itself as they knew it provided shelter, safety, and food for the animals that live there. They wanted to make the loft look like a real rain forest.

Max's enthusiasm for this endeavor grew and grew as his peers, teachers, and parents supported his idea. At home he watched a video and read rain forest books with his parents. Max and his mother, Sandy, began bringing materials to school, providing the whole class with additional information in library books as well as real branches and vines that they gathered from their yard. One day they arrived with a six-foot-long cardboard tube. "This is for our rain forest. It's gonna be a tree, and we need a really big tree so it can be like a real rain forest." Max had a plan, and thus the creation of our own rain forest began.

Many more children became interested and involved in the process of creating our rain forest tree. A tree committee was formed, and we began our discussion in the loft space where we talked about placement of the tree, moving the cardboard tube around in order to determine the desired place for it. The group then moved into the atelier, where the remainder of the tree meetings were to take place. For several weeks children studied, drew, and discussed leaves, plants, and trees to discover the possibilities and design the type of tree they felt would capture and create the vision they had collaboratively developed for the rain forest space.

Ultimately, we decided to make the leaves out of wire and cover them on one side with tissue paper. The branches would be real ones, collected by the children and brought to school. Throughout the process of constructing the tree, children worked together with teachers to continually refine and evaluate progress and to determine whether the tree was turning out the way they had envisioned.

As the leaves and branches were added, one child exclaimed with delight, "It really is starting to look like a real tree!" Another added, "I can't believe we really made this. I never knew we could make such a beautiful tree."

— Evergreen Community School, Santa Monica, Teachers' Documentation of Children's Work

Program Characteristics and Activities

Social studies. The program's approach to social studies is characterized by the following activities:

- Children are encouraged to gain knowledge of the world around them by discussing where places and buildings are, how they get to and from home, how other people get from one place to another, what people do during the day, whether members of their families live near or far from them, and other similar aspects of their world.

- The class goes on field trips by foot to learn about different aspects of the neighborhood.

- Bulletin boards and other displays to which children contribute show positive images and stories of their families, friends, and acquaintances. The teacher encourages children to recognize and accept the many ways in which families are both similar and different.

Science. Driven by curiosity, children explore and learn about the natural world around them; for example, plants, animals, birds, insects, rocks, shells, and pine cones. A preschool program that develops children's interest in science is characterized by the following activities:

- Exploration of the outdoor environment to find, identify, and examine plants, animals, leaves, and other natural phenomena is a regular part of the curriculum.

- The program offers a wide variety of materials for science study, such as seeds to plant, a fish tank or terrarium, a magnifying glass, scales, and mirrors.

- The teacher encourages children to develop and explore scientific hypotheses by observing natural phenomena and events and asking questions, such as, "What are some reasons that you think this happens?" "What do you think would be different if you changed . . . ?" "How could you find out what would happen if . . . ?"

Creative arts. A quality preschool program that offers children a variety of arts to explore is characterized by the following:

- The program emphasizes a wide range of creative arts, including music, dramatic expression, the visual arts, and dance.

- The program emphasizes the process more than the end product. The teacher stresses that there is no one correct way to do artwork or express oneself creatively. Children are encouraged to do their own individual creative work, not to copy a sample presented by the teacher.

- Children are encouraged to appreciate the arts both as participants and as part of an audience.

- The teacher shares his or her own pleasure and skill in artistic expression (e.g., through singing songs or playing a musical instrument).

- The program provides a wide variety of materials for artistic and imaginative expression. These include patterns and cloth from different cultures, large pots of paint, crayons, easels, large sheets of paper, clay, play dough, musical instruments, clothes and hats for dress-up play, and materials from the outdoors (e.g., flowers and leaves).

- Many different forms of children's art are carefully and proudly displayed at the child's eye level.

GOALS OF MUSIC EDUCATION

Music education for young children aims to teach them skills compatible with the ages of young children and their developmental stages of learning. Expected skills include the following:

1. Learn to sing with others.
2. Learn to respond rhythmically to music through creative movement and instrumental expression.
3. Learn to play simple instruments that do not require fine motor skills.
4. Learn to develop attentive listening habits.

These musical skills, nurtured, extended, refined, and developed as the child grows might serve as reasonable objectives for an early childhood music curriculum. . . . The early childhood years are increasingly being recognized as critical years for many aspects of musical growth.

— Adapted from D. T. McDonald, *Music in Our Lives*

Nutrition and health. The program's approach to nutrition and health is characterized by the following:

- The program incorporates an emphasis on nutrition and health by focusing on everyday routines, such as cooking, washing hands, and brushing teeth.

- Children have many opportunities to learn about and eat healthy foods and snacks.

- Children begin identifying the food groups, tasting foods from each group, and learning how each of the food groups helps a body to grow.

- Preparation of snacks and other food is combined with language/literacy and mathematical activities. For example, the teacher uses food preparation as an opportunity to develop children's vocabulary, recognition of printed letters and words, and skills in counting and one-to-one correspondence.

Publications for Other Content Areas

Teachers need to be aware of the expectations for children in kindergarten identified in the publications from the California Department of Education, which are listed on the next page. Teachers view children's early explorations of these subjects as the foundation for later learning in kindergarten and the primary grades. Complete citations for the following titles are in the references section, which appears at the end of this publication.

Health Education

Challenge Standards for Student Success: Health Education, 1998a

History–Social Science

History–Social Science Content Standards for California Public Schools, Kindergarten Through Grade Twelve, 2000a

History–Social Science Framework for California Public Schools, Kindergarten Through Grade Twelve, 1997b

Science

Science Content Standards for California Public Schools, Kindergarten Through Grade Twelve, 2000b

Science Framework for California Public Schools, Kindergarten Through Grade Twelve, 1990

Visual and Performing Arts

Challenge Standards for Student Success: Visual and Performing Arts, 1998b

Visual and Performing Arts Framework for California Public Schools, Kindergarten Through Grade Twelve, 1996c

PART THREE
Resources

Organizations
Further Reading
Program Quality Standards
References

Organizations

T HE ORGANIZATIONS LISTED IN THIS SECTION PROVIDE RESOURCES THAT cover a wide range of topics in early childhood education. These resources are available in various formats: print, video, or electronic.

California Child Care Healthline
1322 Webster St., Suite 402
Oakland, CA 94612-3218
Telephone: (800) 333-3212
Web site: *www.childcarehealth.org*

This toll-free Healthline was created for the use of all child care center staff, family child care providers, and parents who use child care settings in California. The Healthline is staffed by public health nurses experienced in child care and infants' health. The Healthline provides consultation on concerns dealing with special needs, behavioral health, nutrition, car seat safety, and infant and toddler behavior. Other services include workshops and technical assistance for child care providers and agencies.

California Child Care Resource and Referral Network
111 New Montgomery St., 7th Floor
San Francisco, CA 94105
Telephone: (415) 882-0234
Web site: *http://www.rrnetwork.org*

The California Child Care Resource and Referral Network was founded in 1980 as an association of resource and referral (R&R) agencies throughout the state. These R&Rs have grown into comprehensive agencies equipped to provide information, training, and support for parents, caregivers, other community-based agencies, employers, and government policymakers.

California Department of Education
CDE Press/Publications Division, Sales Office
P.O. Box 271
Sacramento, CA 95812-0271
Telephone: (800) 995-4099
Fax: (916) 323-0823
Web site: *http://www.cde.ca.gov/cdepress*

The *Educational Resources Catalog* from CDE Press contains information about publications, such as model curriculum standards; child development materials, which cover general curriculum, quality review, school-age care, special needs, and infant/toddler caregivers; and parent resources. The catalog may be ordered by telephone or through the web site.

California Instructional Technology Clearinghouse
1100 H Street
Modesto, CA 95354
Telephone: (209) 525-4979
Fax: (209) 525-4689
Web site: *http://clearinghouse.k12.ca.us*

The clearinghouse provides descriptions and ratings of educational software for children by age group and links software programs to California educational frameworks and standards.

California Reading Association
3186 D-1 Airway
Costa Mesa, CA 92626
Telephone: (714) 435-1983
Web site: *www.californiareads.org*

This professional organization offers publications, professional development and networking, and updated information on policy issues.

California Tomorrow
436 14th Street, Suite 820
Oakland, CA 94612
Telephone: (510) 496-0220
Web site: *www.californiatomorrow.org*

California Tomorrow, a nonprofit organization, conducts research, provides technical assistance to educators and others, and produces publications, focusing on building a fair and equitable multiracial and multicultural society.

Child Care Law Center
22 Second Street, 5th Floor
San Francisco, CA 94105
Telephone: (415) 495-5498
E-mail: *info@childcarelaw.org*
Web site: *www.childcarelaw.org*

The Child Care Law Center uses legal tools to make high-quality, affordable child care available to every child of every age, family, and community.

Children Now
Telephone: (800) CHILD-44
Web site: *www.childrennow.org*

Children Now is a national organization that promotes community action and policy changes to improve children's quality of life, with special emphasis on poor and at-risk children. Each year Children Now publishes a "report card" on family economics, health, education, and safety. Branches of this organization are located in the following cities:

> **Bay Area of California**
> 1212 Broadway, 5th Floor
> Oakland, CA 94612
> Telephone: (510) 763-2444
> E-mail: *children@childrennow.org*

Los Angeles
2001 South Barrington Ave., Suite 100
Los Angeles, CA 90025
Telephone: (310) 268-2444
E-mail: *cnla@earthlink.net*

New York
355 Lexington Ave., 11th Floor
New York, NY 10017
Telephone: (212) 682-1896
E-mail: *children@inch.com*

Council for Exceptional Children
CEC Publications
1920 Association Drive, Dept. K9032
Reston, VA 20191-1589
Telephone: (888) 232-7733
Web site: *www.cec.sped.org*

The Council for Exceptional Children (CEC) is an international professional organization dedicated to improving educational outcomes for individuals with exceptionalities, students with disabilities, and the gifted. CEC publishes journals, newsletters, and special education materials.

ERIC Clearinghouse on Elementary and Early Childhood Education
University of Illinois at Urbana-Champaign
51 Gerty Drive
Champaign, IL 61820-7469
Telephone: (800) 583-4135
E-mail: *askeece@uiuc.edu*
Web site: *www.ericeece.org/*

The ERIC Clearinghouse provides resources for educators in early childhood and elementary education. It maintains a database of research articles and papers on theory, practice, and policy for early childhood and elementary education and provides, at no cost, digests of useful articles for parents and teachers. An interactive web site for educators is available.

Family Resource Coalition
200 South Michigan Avenue, Suite 1520
Chicago, IL 60604
Telephone: (312) 341-0900

This organization gives information on parenting and starting parent support groups.

National Association for the Education of Young Children
1509 16th Street, NW
Washington, DC 20036-1426
Telephone: (800) 424-2460
Web site: *www.naeyc.org*

The association's *Early Childhood Resources Catalog* contains listings of materials covering all topics included in the *Prekindergarten Learning and Development Guidelines.* The catalog may be ordered by telephone or through the web site.

National Child Care Information Center
243 Church Street, NW, 2nd Floor
Vienna, VA 22180
Telephone: (800) 616-2242
Fax: (800) 716-2242
TTY: (800) 516-2242
Web site: *www.nccic.org/abtnccic.html*

The center's activities include dissemination of child care information, publication of the *Child Care Bulletin*, child care linkages, state technical assistance, and national leadership forums.

Office of Educational Research and Improvement Research Projects

The Office of Educational Research and Improvement (OERI) has funded three projects that have produced articles and reports in specific areas of child development and early childhood education. Some of these materials may be downloaded from the Internet. Information on these projects follows:

Center for Research on Education, Diversity, and Excellence
University of California, Santa Cruz
1156 High Street
Santa Cruz, CA 95064
Telephone: (408) 459-3500
Director: Roland Tharp
OERI contact: Gilbert N. Garcia (202) 219-2144
Web site: *www.crede.ucsc.edu*

Center for the Improvement of Early Reading Achievement
University of Michigan
School of Education
610 E. University Avenue, Room 1600 SEB
Ann Arbor, MI 48109-1259
Telephone: (734) 647-6940
Director: Elfrieda H. Hiebert
OERI contact: Anne P. Sweet (202) 219-2043
Web site: *www.ciera.org*

National Center for Early Development and Learning
Frank Porter Graham Child Development Center
University of North Carolina, Chapel Hill
CB#4100
Chapel Hill, NC 27599-4100
Telephone: (919) 966-4250
Director: Don Bailey
OERI contact: Naomi Karp (202) 219-1586
Web site: *www.fpg.unc.edu*

Protection and Advocacy, Inc.
449 15th Street, Suite 401
Oakland, CA 94612-2821
Telephone: (800) 776-5746
Web site: *www.pai-ca.org*

This organization provides legal and other advice to families of children with special needs.

Further Reading

 RESOURCES FOR MORE INFORMATION ON EACH OF THE TOPICS DISCUSSED throughout this publication appear in this section.

Teaching and Learning

California Department of Education. 1999. *First Class: A Guide for Early Primary Education.* Sacramento: California Department of Education.

Carter, R. 1998. *Mapping the Mind.* Berkeley: University of California Press.

Edwards, C.; L. Gandini; and G. Forman. 1998. *The Hundred Languages of Children: The Reggio Emilia Approach to Early Childhood Education* (Second edition). Norwood, N.J.: Ablex.

Griffin, E. F. 1999. *Island of Childhood: Education in the Special World of Nursery School.* Troy, N.Y.: Educator's International Press.

Jones, E., and G. Reynolds. 1992. *The Play's the Thing: Teachers' Roles in Children's Play.* New York: Teachers College Press.

National Association for the Education of Young Children. 1997. *Developmentally Appropriate Practice in Early Childhood Programs* (Revised edition). Edited by S. Bredekamp and C. Copple. Washington, D.C.: National Association for the Education of Young Children.

National Educational Goals Panel. 1995. *Reconsidering Children's Early Development and Learning: Toward Common Views and Vocabulary.* Edited by S. L. Kagan, E. Moore, and S. Bredekamp. Washington, D.C.: U.S. Government Printing Office.

Paley, V. G. 1993. *You Can't Say You Can't Play.* Cambridge, Mass.: Harvard University Press.

Smilansky, S., and L. Shafatya. 1990. *Facilitating Play.* Gaithersburg, Md.: Psychosocial and Educational Publications.

Note: The publication data in this section were supplied by the Child Development Division, California Department of Education. Questions about the references should be addressed to that office; telephone (916) 323-5089.

Program Foundations

Resources are provided for the following topics in Chapter 5, "Program Foundations": "Planning the Preschool Environment," "Addressing Cultural Diversity," "Planning for Assessment," "Including Children with Disabilities or Other Special Needs," "Involving Parents and Families," and "Organizing Staff Preparation and Development Programs."

Planning the Preschool Environment

Harms, T.; R. M. Clifford; and D. Cryer. 1998. *Early Childhood Environment Rating Scale* (Revised edition). New York: Teachers College Press.

Addressing Cultural Diversity

Chang, H. N., and L. Sakai. 1993. *Affirming Children's Roots: Cultural and Linguistic Diversity in Early Care and Education.* San Francisco: California Tomorrow.

Derman-Sparks, L. 1989. *Anti-Bias Curriculum: Tools for Empowering Young Children.* Washington, D.C.: National Association for the Education of Young Children.

Garcia, E. E., and others. 1995. "Meeting the Challenge of Linguistic and Cultural Diversity in Early Childhood Education," in *Yearbook in Early Childhood Education,* Vol. 6. New York: Teachers College Press.

Gonzalez-Mena, J. 1993. *Multicultural Issues in Child Care.* Mountain View, Calif.: Mayfield Publishing Company.

Kendall, F. 1996. *Diversity in the Classroom: New Approaches to the Education of Young Children* (Second edition). Early Childhood Education Series. New York: Teachers College Press.

National Association for the Education of Young Children. 1992. *Alike and Different: Exploring Our Humanity with Young Children.* Edited by B. Neugebauer. Washington, D.C.: National Association for the Education of Young Children.

Nieto, S. 1999. *The Light in Their Eyes: Creating Multicultural Learning Communities.* New York: Teachers College Press.

Planning for Assessment

High/Scope Educational Research Foundation. 1999. *Child Observation Record.* Ypsilanti, Mich.: High/Scope Press.

Meisels, S. J., and others. 1995. *The Work Sampling System: An Overview.* Ann Arbor, Mich.: Rebus Planning Associates, Inc.

National Association for the Education of Young Children. 1992. *Reaching Potentials: Appropriate Curriculum and Assessment for Young Children,* Vol. 1. Edited by S. Bredekamp and T. Rosegrant. Washington, D.C.: National Association for the Education of Young Children.

Including Children with Disabilities or Other Special Needs

California Department of Education. 1994. *Just Kids: A Practical Guide for Working with Children Prenatally Substance-Exposed.* Sacramento: California Department of Education.

California Department of Education. 1996. *Project EXCEPTIONAL: A Guide for Training and Recruiting Child Care Providers to Serve Young Children with Disabilities.* In two volumes. Edited by L. Cranor and A. Kuschner. Sacramento: California Department of Education.
(Volume 1 covers methods and strategies for daily work with children with disabilities and their families, including legal, insurance, and confidentiality issues. Volume 2 is a practical guide to recruiting and training child care providers to work with children with disabilities.)

California Department of Education. 1999. *Early Warning Signs That Your Child May Need Help.* Sacramento: California Department of Education.
(Also available in Chinese, Spanish, and Vietnamese versions.)

California Department of Education. 2000. *California Special Education Programs: A Composite of Laws.* Sacramento: California Department of Education.
(This publication is updated annually.)

Council for Exceptional Children. 1993. *DEC Recommended Practices: Indicators of Quality in Programs for Infants and Young Children with Special Needs and Their Families.* Reston, Va.: Council for Exceptional Children, Division of Early Childhood.

National Association for the Education of Young Children. 1992. *Reaching Potentials: Appropriate Curriculum and Assessment for Young Children,* Vol. 1. Edited by S. Bredekamp and T. Rosegrant. Washington, D.C.: National Association for the Education of Young Children.

National Association for the Education of Young Children. 1994. *Including Children with Special Needs in Early Childhood Programs.* Edited by M. Wolery and J. S. Wilbers. Washington, D.C.: National Association for the Education of Young Children.

National Association for the Education of Young Children. 1999. *When Teachers Reflect: Journeys Toward Effective, Inclusive Practice.* Edited by W. A. Tertell, S. M. Klein, and J. L. Jewett. Washington, D.C.: National Association for the Education of Young Children.

Involving Parents and Families

Anderson, M. P. 1998. *Families Matter: Parent–Provider Partnerships.* Cambridge, Mass.: Harvard Family Research Project.

Lee, L., and E. Selderman. 1998. *Families Matter: The Parent Services Project.* Cambridge, Mass.: Harvard Family Research Project.

National Association for the Education of Young Children. 1997. *Family-Friendly Communications for Early Childhood Programs.* Edited by D. Diffily and K. Morrison. Washington, D.C.: National Association for the Education of Young Children.

Putting Families First: America's Family Support Movement and the Challenge of Change. 1994. Edited by S. L. Kagan and B. Weissbourd. San Francisco: Jossey-Bass.

Valdés, G. 1996. *Con Respeto: Bridging the Distances Between Culturally Diverse Families and Schools.* New York: Teachers College Press.

Washington, V.; V. Johnson; and J. B. McCracken. 1995. *Grassroots Success: Preparing Schools and Families for Each Other.* Washington, D.C.: National Association for the Education of Young Children.

Organizing Staff Preparation and Development Programs

Advancing Careers in Child Development. 1999. *Competencies for the Various Levels of the Child Development Permit* (1999 Revised edition). Pasadena, Calif.: Pacific Oaks College.

Bellm, D.; M. Whitebook; and P. Hnatiuk. 1997. *The Early Childhood Mentoring Curriculum: A Handbook for Mentors.* Washington, D.C.: Center for the Child Care Workforce.

Bellm, D.; M. Whitebook; and P. Hnatiuk. 1997. *The Early Childhood Mentoring Curriculum: Trainer's Guide.* Washington, D.C.: Center for the Child Care Workforce.

Bloom, J. 1997. *A Great Place to Work: Improving Conditions for Staff in Young Children's Programs* (Revised edition). Washington, D.C.: National Association for the Education of Young Children.

Whitebook, M., and D. Bellm. 1999. *Taking on Turnover: An Action Guide for Child Care Center Teachers and Directors.* Washington, D.C.: Center for the Child Care Workforce.

Curriculum

Resources are provided for the following topics in Chapter 6, "Curriculum": "Social and Emotional Development," "Language and Literacy Development," "Mathematics Learning and Development," "Physical and Motor Development," and "Other Curriculum Content Areas."

Social and Emotional Development

California Department of Education. 1997. *Continuity for Young Children: Positive Transitions to Elementary School.* Sacramento: California Department of Education.

California Department of Education. 1997. *Reducing Exceptional Stress and Trauma: Curriculum and Intervention Guidelines.* Sacramento: California Department of Education.

DeVries, R., and B. Zan. 1994. *Moral Classrooms, Moral Children: Creating a Constructivist Atmosphere in Early Education.* New York: Teachers College Press.

Goulet, M. 1999. *How Caring Relationships Support Self-Regulation.* 68 min. Washington, D.C.: National Association for the Education of Young Children. Videotape.

Katz, L. G., and D. E. McClellan. 1997. *Fostering Children's Social Competence: The Teacher's Role.* Washington, D.C.: National Association for the Education of Young Children.

Lewis, C. C. 1995. *Educating Hearts and Minds: Reflections on Japanese Preschool and Elementary Education.* New York: Cambridge University Press.

Language and Literacy Development

California Department of Education. 1995. *Every Child a Reader: The Report of the California Reading Task Force.* Sacramento: California Department of Education.

California Department of Education. 1996. *Teaching Reading: A Balanced, Comprehensive Approach to Teaching Reading in Prekindergarten Through Grade Three.* Sacramento: California Department of Education.

California Department of Education. 1998. *Assessing and Fostering the Development of a First and a Second Language in Early Childhood: Training Manual.* Sacramento: California Department of Education.

California Department of Education. 1998. *Assessing the Development of a First and a Second Language in Early Childhood: Resource Guide.* Sacramento: California Department of Education.

California Department of Education. 1998. *Fostering the Development of a First and a Second Language in Early Childhood: Resource Guide.* Sacramento: California Department of Education.

California Department of Education. 1998. *Observing Preschoolers: Assessing First and Second Language Development.* 30 min. Sacramento: California Department of Education. Videotape.

California Department of Education. 1998. *Talking with Preschoolers: Strategies for Promoting First and Second Language Development.* 30 min. Sacramento: California Department of Education. Videotape.

California Department of Education. 1999. *Reading/Language Arts Framework for California Public Schools, Kindergarten Through Grade Twelve.* Sacramento: California Department of Education.

National Association for the Education of Young Children and International Reading Association. 1998. "Learning to Read and Write: Developmentally Appropriate Practices for Young Children," *Young Children*, 53 (47), 30–46.

National Research Council. 1999. *Starting Out Right: A Guide to Promoting Children's Reading Success.* Edited by M. S. Burns, P. Griffin, and C. E. Snow. Washington, D.C.: National Academy Press.

Mathematics Learning and Development

California Department of Education. 1999. *Mathematics Framework for California Public Schools, Kindergarten Through Grade Twelve.* Sacramento: California Department of Education.

Clements, D. H. 1999. "Playing Math with Young Children," *Curriculum Administrator*, 35 (4), 25–28.

Coates, G. D., and V. Thompson. 1999. "Involving Parents of Four- and Five-Year-Olds in Their Children's Mathematics Education: The Family Math Experience," in *Mathematics in the Early Years.* Edited by Juanita V. Copely. Reston, Va.: National Council of Teachers of Mathematics; Washington, D.C.: National Association for the Education of Young Children.

Dutton, W. H.; A. Dutton; and B. Dutton. 1996. *Mathematics Children Use and Understand.* Napa, Calif.: Rattle OK Publications.

Fromboluti, C. S., and N. Rinck. 1999. *Early Childhood: Where Learning Begins—Mathematics.* Washington, D.C.: U.S. Department of Education, Office of Educational Research and Improvement.

Kamii, C. 1995. *Number in Preschool and Kindergarten.* Washington, D.C.: National Association for the Education of Young Children.

Miller, D., and A. McKinnon. 1995. *The Beginning School Mathematics Project.* Alexandria, Va.: Association for Supervision and Curriculum Development.

National Council of Teachers of Mathematics and National Association for the Education of Young Children. *Mathematics in the Early Years.* 1999. Edited by Juanita V. Copely. Reston, Va.: National Council of Teachers of Mathematics; Washington, D.C.: National Association for the Education of Young Children.

Shane, R. 1999. "Making Connections: A 'Number Curriculum' for Preschoolers," in *Mathematics in the Early Years*. Edited by Juanita V. Copely. Reston, Va.: National Council of Teachers of Mathematics; Washington, D.C.: National Association for the Education of Young Children.

Physical and Motor Development

California Department of Education. 1995. *Keeping Kids Healthy: Preventing and Managing Communicable Disease in Child Care*. Sacramento: California Department of Education.

California Department of Education. 1995. *Keeping Kids Healthy: Preventing and Managing Communicable Disease in Child Care*. 30 min. Sacramento: California Department of Education. Videotape.

Early Childhood Education Linkage System. 1997. *Model Child Care Health Policies* (Revised 1997). Washington, D.C.: National Association for the Education of Young Children.

Halverson, L. E. 1994. "The Significance of the Young Child's Motor Development." Proceedings of a conference sponsored by the American Association for Health, Physical Education, and Recreation and the National Association for the Education of Young Children. Washington, D.C.

National Educational Goals Panel. 1995. *Reconsidering Children's Early Development and Learning: Toward Common Views and Vocabulary*. Edited by S. L. Kagan, E. Moore, and S. Bredekamp. Washington, D.C.: U.S. Government Printing Office.

Other Curriculum Content Areas

California Department of Education. 1997. *Arts Work—A Call for Arts Education for All California Students*. The Report of the Superintendent's Task Force on the Visual and Performing Arts. Sacramento: California Department of Education.

Engel, B. S. 1995. *Considering Children's Art: Why and How to Value Their Works*. Washington, D.C.: National Association for the Education of Young Children.

ERIC/EECE. 1996. *The Project Approach Catalog*. Edited by J. J. Helm. Champaign, Ill.: ERIC Clearinghouse on Elementary and Early Childhood Education.

ERIC/EECE. 1998. *The Project Approach Catalog 2*. Edited by J. J. Helm. Champaign, Ill.: ERIC Clearinghouse on Elementary and Early Childhood Education.

Fromboluti, C. S., and C. Seefeldt. 1999. *Early Childhood: Where Learning Begins—Geography*. Washington, D.C.: U.S. Department of Education, Office of Educational Research and Improvement.

Holt, B. G. 1993. *Science with Young Children*. Washington, D.C.: National Association for the Education of Young Children.

Young Children and the Arts: Making Creative Connections—A Report on the Task Force on Children's Learning and the Arts: Birth to Eight. 1998. Washington, D.C.: Council of Chief State School Officers, Arts Education Partnership.

Technology

Bowman, B. 1990. "Technology in Early Childhood Education," in *Technology in Today's Schools*, 129–41. Edited by C. Warger. Alexandria, Va.: Association for Supervision and Curriculum Development.

Children's Software Revue. Edited by W. Buckleitner. Web site: *www.childrenssoftware.com.* (The mailing address for this newsletter is 44 Main St., Flemington, NJ 08822.)

Clements, D.; B. Nastasi; and S. Swaminathan. 1993. "Young Children and Computers: Crossroads and Directions from Research," *Young Children,* 48 (2), 56–64.

Davidson, J. 1990. *Children and Computers Together in the Early Childhood Classroom.* New York: Delmar.

ERIC/EECE. 1995. *A to Z: The Early Childhood Educator's Guide to the Internet.* Champaign, Ill.: ERIC Clearinghouse on Elementary and Early Childhood Education.

Haugland, S. W., and J. L. Wright. 1997. *Young Children and Technology: A World of Discovery.* Needham Heights, Mass.: Allyn and Bacon.

Holder-Brown, L., and H. P. Howard. 1992. "Children with Disabilities Who Use Assistive Technology: Ethical Considerations," *Young Children,* 47 (6), 73–77.

National Association for the Education of Young Children. 1994. *Young Children: Active Learners in a Technological Age.* Edited by J. L. Wright and D. D. Shade. Washington, D.C.: National Association for the Education of Young Children.

National Association for the Education of Young Children. 1996. "NAEYC Position Statement: Technology and Young Children: Ages Three Through Eight," *Young Children,* 51 (6), 11–16. (This position paper may be found on the Web site for NAEYC: *http://www.naeyc.org/about/about_index.htm.)*

Shade, D. 1997. *Computers in Early Childhood: A World of Discovery.* New York: Prentice Hall.

Research on Brain Development

Diamond, M., and J. Hopson. 1998. *Magic Trees of the Mind: How to Nurture Your Child's Intelligence, Creativity, and Healthy Emotions from Birth Through Adolescence.* New York: E. P. Dutton.

Greenspan, S. I. 1997. *The Growth of the Mind and the Endangered Origins of Intelligence.* Reading, Mass.: Addison Wesley.

Kotulak, R. 1997. *Inside the Brain: Revolutionary Discoveries of How the Mind Works.* Kansas City, Mo.: Andrews McMeel Publishing.

Ramey, C. T., and S. L. Ramey. 1999. *Right from Birth: Building Your Child's Foundation for Life.* New York: Goddard Press.

Shore, R. 1997. *Rethinking the Brain: New Insights into Early Development.* New York: Families and Work Institute.

Wolfe, P., and R. Brandt. 1998. "What Do We Know from Brain Research?" *Educational Leadership.* (November), 8–12.

Program Quality

Burton, A., and M. Whitebook. 1998. *Child Care Staff Compensation Guidelines for California 1998.* Washington, D.C.: Center for the Child Care Workforce.

Koralek, D.; L. Coker; and D. Dodge. 1993. *The What, Why, and How of High-Quality Early Childhood Education: A Guide for On-Site Supervision.* Washington, D.C.: National Association for the Education of Young Children.

National Association for the Education of Young Children. 1996. *NAEYC Accreditation: A Decade of Learning and the Years Ahead.* Edited by S. Bredekamp and B. Willer. Washington, D.C.: National Association for the Education of Young Children.

National Association for the Education of Young Children. 1998. *Accreditation Criteria and Procedures of the National Association for the Education of Young Children* (Revised edition). Washington, D.C.: National Association for the Education of Young Children.

Web Sites

AbleData: *www.abledata.com*

Alliance for Technology Access: *www.ataccess.org*

Assistive Technology Funding and Systems Change Project: *www.ucpa.org/html/innovative/atfsc_index.html*

Augmentative/Alternative Communication Resource: *www.aacintervention.com*

California Assistive Technology System (TECH Act Project): *www.catsca.org*

California Consortium to Prevent Child Abuse: *www.ccpca.org*

California Department of Education: *http://www.cde.ca.gov*

California Department of Education, Desired Results: *http://www.cde.ca.gov/cyfsbranch/child_development/DR2.htm*

California Department of Education, Ed-data: *www.ed-data.k12.ca.us/*

Center for Applied Special Technology (CAST): *www.cast.org*

Children, Youth, and Families Education and Research Network: *www.cyfernet.org/*

Children's Software Revue: *www.childrenssoftware.com*

Children's Television Workshop: *www.ctw.org*

Dreamms for Kids, Inc.: *www.dreamms.org*

Early Childhood Education: *www.worldvillage.com/ideabox/index.html*

Early Childhood Today: *www.place.scholastic.com/ect/index.html*

Families and Work Institute: *www.families and work.org*

Family World: *www.family.disney.com*

High/Scope Education Foundation: *www.highscope.org*

Juniornet: *www.juniornet.com*

Marc's Special Education Home Page: *www.halcyon.com/marcs/sped.html*

National Association for the Education of Young Children: *www.naeyc.org*

National Early Childhood Technical Assistance System (NEC*TAS): *www.nectas.unc.edu*

Internet Discussion Groups for Early Childhood Educators

Early Childhood Education Network. *ECENET-L@postoffice.cso.uiuc.edu* (For more information contact *ericeece@uiuc.edu*.)

Early Childhood Educators Online. *ECEOL-L@postoffice.cso.uiuc.edu* (For more information contact *bonnieb@maine.bitnet*.)

Program Quality Standards

RESCHOOL EDUCATION IN CALIFORNIA CAN BE STRENGTHENED BY THE adoption of California and national standards of quality. Major sources of quality standards in early childhood education appear in this section.

Resources for Prekindergarten and the Primary Grades

The Reading Task Force that developed *Every Child a Reader* called for a balanced, comprehensive approach to early reading instruction that includes both teacher-directed skills instruction and the activities and strategies most often associated with literature-based, integrated language arts instruction. It addresses prekindergarten through grade three.

Every Child a Reader: The Report of the California Reading Task Force. 1995. Sacramento: California Department of Education.

More information on this publication is available from:

CDE Press
California Department of Education
CDE Press, Sales Office
P.O. Box 271
Sacramento, CA 95812-0271
Telephone: (916) 445-1260; (800) 995-4099

The Desired Results for Children and Families web site provides an overview of the background, purpose, and components of the Desired Results System.

"Desired Results for Children and Families." Forthcoming. Sacramento: California Department of Education.

More information is available from:

California Department of Education
Child Development Division
P.O. Box 944272
Sacramento, CA 94244-2720
(916) 323-5089
Web site: *http://www.cde.ca.gov/cyfsbranch/child_development/DR2.htm*

The *Early Childhood Environment Rating Scale (ECERS)* is a widely used program quality assessment instrument designed for use in preschool, kindergarten, and child care programs serving children aged two and one-half through five years. Developed at the Frank Porter Graham Child Development Center at the University of North Carolina, Chapel Hill, the *ECERS* was revised and updated in 1998 to include greater emphasis on cultural diversity, family concerns, and individual children's needs. The new version is known as *ECERS-R*.

ECERS-R addresses the following content areas: space and furnishings, personal care routines, language-reasoning, activities, interaction, program structure, and parents and staff.

Both the reliability and the validity of the *ECERS-R* are well established; therefore, the instrument can be used with confidence that positive results indicate good program quality. The instrument is self-administering, meaning that a program director can assess his or her own program, or it can be used by outside observers of the program. A video training package for the *ECERS-R* is available from Teachers College Press for use in self-instruction or as part of group training.

Harms, T.; R. M. Clifford; and D. Cryer. *Early Childhood Environment Rating Scale* (Revised edition). 1998. New York: Teachers College Press.

A companion instrument for family child care is:

Harms, T., and R. M. Clifford. *Family Day Care Rating Scale (FACERS)*. 1989. New York: Teachers College Press.

More information on these materials is available from:

Teachers College Press
Teachers College, Columbia University
1234 Amsterdam Avenue
New York, NY 10027

California Commission on Teacher Credentialing

Since its inception in 1970, the California Commission on Teacher Credentialing has supported and encouraged the professional development of all educators. An educator's growth is valued as a mark of professional stature and as a source and a stimulant of student growth and achievement. The Commission believes that "learning students" are most likely to be found in the presence of "learning teachers" and other educators.

The manual titled *The California Professional Growth Manual for Child Development Permits* is available from the Commission on Teacher Credentialing. This document provides information for holders of the Child Development Permit on how to renew their permit. It also provides information for professional growth advisers, defined as an individual who advises permit holders regarding their professional growth and development. It includes information on all levels of the permit, renewal requirements, selection of a professional growth adviser, and the stages in the professional growth cycle.

The California Professional Growth Manual for Child Development Permits. 1999. Sacramento: California Commission on Teacher Credentialing. (This publication is available in English and Spanish.)

More information on this publication is available from:

California Commission on Teacher Credentialing
1900 Capitol Avenue
Sacramento, CA 95814-4213
Telephone: (916) 445-7254
Fax: (916) 327-3166
Web site: *http://www.ctc.ca.gov*

National Association for the Education of Young Children

The National Association for the Education of Young Children (NAEYC), the nation's largest organization of early childhood educators, has established an accreditation program through its National Academy of Early Childhood Programs. This program is a national voluntary accreditation system for all types of preschools, kindergartens, child care centers, and school-age child care programs. As of spring 2000, more than 7,000 programs serving a half-million children achieved NAEYC accreditation, and an additional 12,000 programs are in the process of being accredited.

The accreditation process consists of an extensive self-study. The accuracy of the program's self-study is subsequently verified by a team of trained volunteer validators. The validated self-study, including the program director's responses to the validation visit, is then reviewed by a three-member national commission composed of recognized experts in child care and early childhood education. On the basis of their review, these experts judge whether the program is in substantial compliance with the academy's criteria and grants accreditation for three years. Finally, the early childhood program agrees to act on the commission's suggestions regarding areas needing improvement and to submit annual reports.

The accreditation process examines whether the program offers:

◆ A curriculum based on sound principles of child development

◆ High-quality interactions among children and staff

◆ A healthy, safe environment for children

◆ A sufficient number of adults per children in group sizes appropriate for children's ages

◆ Strong communication among parents and staff

◆ More involvement by early childhood professionals in decision making

◆ A commitment to the continual development of teaching skills among staff

Overall, the greatest emphasis is placed on:

◆ The quality of interactions among staff and children

◆ The developmental appropriateness of the curriculum

More information on NAEYC's accreditation program is available from:

National Association for the Education of Young Children
National Academy of Early Childhood Programs
1509 16th Street, N.W.
Washington, DC 20036-1426
(202) 232-8777
(800) 424-2460, ext. 360
Web site: *www.naeyc.org*

Content Standards for Kindergarten Through Grade Twelve

Subject-specific content standards for kindergarten through grade twelve have been developed to ensure high quality in content-specific curriculum and instruction. Prekindergarten teachers and staff should be aware of these content standards so that their daily planning will support the development of needed skills and provide opportunities for practice. These publications are listed as follows:

English–Language Arts Content Standards for California Public Schools, Kindergarten Through Grade Twelve. 1998. Sacramento: California Department of Education.

History–Social Science Standards for California Public Schools, Kindergarten Through Grade Twelve. 2000. Sacramento: California Department of Education.

Mathematics Content Standards for California Public Schools, Kindergarten Through Grade Twelve. 1999. Sacramento: California Department of Education.

Science Content Standards for California Public Schools, Kindergarten Through Grade Twelve. 2000. Sacramento: California Department of Education.

These publications are available from the California Department of Education, CDE Press, which may be contacted as follows:

California Department of Education
CDE Press/Publications Division, Sales Unit
P.O. Box 271
Sacramento, CA 95812-0271
Telephone: (916) 445-1260
Fax: (916) 323-0823

Telephone orders will be accepted toll-free (1-800-995-4099) for credit card purchases only.

References

Sources cited in the text appear in this list of references.

Adams, M. J. 1990. *Beginning to Read: Thinking and Learning About Print.* Cambridge: Massachusetts Institute of Technology Press.

Advancing Careers in Child Development. 1999. *Competencies for the Various Levels of the Child Development Permit.* Pasadena, Calif.: Pacific Oaks College.

African American Early Childhood Resource Center. 1998. *Resources to Build Diverse Leadership.* Washington, D.C.: National Black Child Development Institute.

Alexander, K. L, and D. R. Entwisle. 1988. "Achievement in the First Two Years of School: Patterns and Processes," *Monographs of the Society for Research in Child Development,* Vol. 53 (Serial no. 218).

American Academy of Pediatrics. 1987. *Health in Day Care: A Manual for Health Professionals.* Elk Grove, Ill.: American Academy of Pediatrics.

American Public Health Association and American Academy of Pediatrics. 1992. *Caring for Our Children: National Health and Safety Performance Standards—Guidelines for Out-of-Home Child Care Programs.* Washington, D.C.: American Public Health Association; Elk Grove Village, Ill.: American Academy of Pediatrics.

Armistead, M. 1996. "Constructivism and Arts-Based Programs." Paper presented at the National Association of Early Childhood Educators Conference, Minneapolis, Minnesota, June 5.

Armstrong, T. 1994. "The Foundations of the Theory of Multiple Intelligences," in *Multiple Intelligences.* Alexandria, Va.: Association for Supervision and Curriculum Development.

Au, K. 1998. "Social Constructivism and the School: Literacy of Students of Diverse Backgrounds," *Journal of Literacy Research,* 30 (2), 297–313.

Bailey, D. B., and others. 1998. "Inclusion in the Context of Competing Values in Early Childhood Education," *Early Childhood Research Quarterly,* 13, 27–48.

Bailey, D. B., and M. Wolery. 1992. *Teaching Infants and Preschoolers with Disabilities.* Englewood Cliffs, N.J.: Prentice Hall.

Note: The publication data in this section were supplied by the Child Development Division, California Department of Education. Questions about the references should be addressed to that office; telephone (916) 323-5089.

Beilin, H., and A. Klein. 1982. *Strategies and Structures in Understanding Geometry.* Washington, D.C.: National Science Foundation.

Benelli, C., and B. Youngue. 1995. "Supporting Young Children's Motor Skill Development," *Childhood Education* (summer), 217–21.

Berrueta-Clement, J., and others. 1984. *Changed Lives: The Effects of the Perry Preschool Program on Youth Through Age 19.* Ypsilanti, Mich.: High/Scope Educational Research Foundation.

Bondurant-Utz, J. A. 1994. "Cultural Diversity," in *A Practical Guide to Infant and Preschool Assessment in Special Education.* Edited by J. A. Bondurant-Utz and L. B. Luciano. Needham Heights, Mass.: Allyn and Bacon.

Bricker, D. D. 1978. "A Rationale for the Integration of Handicapped and Nonhandicapped Preschool Children," in *Early Intervention and the Integration of Handicapped and Nonhandicapped Children,* 3–26. Edited by M. Guralnick. Baltimore: University Park Press.

Burchinal, M. R., and others. 1996. "Quality of Center Child Care and Infant Cognitive and Language Development," *Child Development,* 67, 606–20.

Burchinal, M. R.; M. Lee; and C. Ramey. 1989. "Type of Day Care and Preschool Intellectual Development in Disadvantaged Children," *Child Development,* 60, 128–37.

Burton, A., and M. Whitebook. 1998. *Child Care Staff Compensation Guidelines for California 1998.* Washington, D.C.: Center for the Child Care Workforce. (Prepared for the California Department of Education)

Bus, A. G.; M. H. van IJzendoorn; and A. D. Pellegrini. 1995. "Joint Book Reading Makes for Success in Learning to Read: A Meta-Analysis on Intergenerational Transmission of Literacy," *Review of Educational Research,* 65 (1), 1–21.

Buysse, V., and D. B. Bailey. 1993. "Behavioral and Developmental Outcomes in Young Children with Disabilities in Integrated and Segregated Settings: A Review of Comparative Studies," *Journal of Special Education,* 26, 434–61.

California Department of Education. 1990. *Science Framework for California Public Schools, Kindergarten Through Grade Twelve.* Sacramento: California Department of Education.

California Department of Education. 1996a. *Project EXCEPTIONAL: A Guide for Training and Recruiting Child Care Providers to Serve Young Children with Disabilities.* Vol. 1. Sacramento: California Department of Education.

California Department of Education. 1996b. *Teaching Reading: A Balanced, Comprehensive Approach to Teaching Reading in Prekindergarten Through Grade Three.* Sacramento: California Department of Education.

California Department of Education. 1996c. *Visual and Performing Arts Framework for California Public Schools, Kindergarten Through Grade Twelve.* Sacramento: California Department of Education.

California Department of Education. 1997a. *Continuity for Young Children: Positive Transitions to Elementary School.* Sacramento: California Department of Education.

California Department of Education. 1997b. *History–Social Science Framework for California Public Schools, Kindergarten Through Grade Twelve.* Sacramento: California Department of Education.

California Department of Education. 1998a. *Challenge Standards for Student Success: Health Education.* Sacramento: California Department of Education.

California Department of Education. 1998b. *Challenge Standards for Student Success: Visual and Performing Arts.* Sacramento: California Department of Education.

California Department of Education. 1998c. *English–Language Arts Content Standards for California Public Schools, Kindergarten Through Grade Twelve.* Sacramento: California Department of Education.

California Department of Education. 1998d. *Fostering the Development of a First and a Second Language in Early Childhood: Resource Guide.* Sacramento: California Department of Education.

California Department of Education. 1998e. *Ready to Learn: Quality Preschools for California in the 21st Century. The Report of the Superintendent's Universal Preschool Task Force.* Sacramento: California Department of Education.

California Department of Education. 1999a. "Finding Daycare for Robert," *Bridges* (spring), 4 (1).

California Department of Education. 1999b. *First Class: A Guide for Early Primary Education.* Sacramento: California Department of Education.

California Department of Education. 1999c. "Map to Services for Children with Special Needs and Their Families," *Bridges,* 4 (1), 20–21.

California Department of Education. 1999d. *Mathematics Content Standards for California Public Schools, Kindergarten Through Grade Twelve.* Sacramento: California Department of Education.

California Department of Education. 1999e. *Mathematics Framework for California Public Schools, Kindergarten Through Grade Twelve.* Sacramento: California Department of Education.

California Department of Education.1999f. *Reading/Language Arts Framework for California Public Schools, Kindergarten Through Grade Twelve.* Sacramento: California Department of Education.

California Department of Education. 2000a. *History–Social Science Content Standards for California Public Schools: Kindergarten Through Grade Twelve.* Sacramento: California Department of Education.

California Department of Education. 2000b. *Science Content Standards for California Public Schools: Kindergarten Through Grade Twelve.* Sacramento: California Department of Education.

California Department of Education. 2000c. *Special Education Rights of Parents and Children Under the Individuals with Disabilities Education Act, Part B.* Sacramento: California Department of Education.

California Institute on Human Services. 1996. *Health and Safety Considerations: Caring for Young Children with Exceptional Health Care Needs.* Edited by L. S. Cranor and A. Kuschner. Rohnert Park, Calif.: Sonoma State University.

California Institute on Human Services. 1998. *CONNECTIONS Project: Learning Communities for All Children—Training Manual.* Rohnert Park, Calif.: Sonoma State University.

Campbell, F. A., and C. Ramey. 1994. "Effects of Early Intervention on Intellectual and Academic Achievement: A Follow-Up Study of Children from Low-Income Families," *Child Development,* 65, 669–84.

Campbell, F. A., and C. Ramey. 1999. *Early Learning, Later Success: The Abecedarian Study.* Chapel Hill, N.C.: University of North Carolina, Chapel Hill. Frank Porter Graham Child Development Center.

Carnegie Task Force on Meeting the Needs of Young Children. 1994. *Starting Points: Meeting the Needs of Our Youngest Children.* New York: Carnegie Corporation of New York.

Carter, M. 1999. "Making Learning Visible," *Child Care Information and Exchange* (July), 35–37.

Chang, H. N., and L. Sakai. 1993. *Affirming Children's Roots: Cultural and Linguistic Diversity in Early Care and Education.* San Francisco: California Tomorrow.

Children Now. 1999. *California Report Card 1999: How Our Youngest Children Are Faring.* Oakland, Calif.: Children Now.

Clay, M. M. 1979. *What Did I Write? Beginning Writing Behavior.* Portsmouth, N.H.: Heinemann Educational Books, Inc.

Clements, D. H. 1994. "The Uniqueness of the Computer as a Learning Tool: Insights from Research and Practice," in *Young Children: Active Learners in a Technological Age,* 31–49. Edited by J. L. Wright and D. D. Shade. Washington, D.C.: National Association for the Education of Young Children.

Clements, D. H. 1999. "Playing Math with Young Children," *Curriculum Administrator,* 35 (4), 25–28.

Clements, D. H., and M. T. Battista. 1992. "Geometry and Spatial Reasoning," in *Handbook of Research on Mathematics Teaching and Learning,* 420–64. Edited by D. Grouws. New York: Macmillan.

Cohen, L., and others. 1996. *Child Development, Health, and Safety: Educational Materials for Home Visitors and Parents.* Gaithersburg, Md.: Aspen Publishers.

Cole, M., and S. Cole. 1993. *The Development of Children.* New York: Scientific American Books.

Council for Exceptional Children. 1993. *DEC Recommended Practices: Indicators of Quality in Programs for Infants and Young Children with Special Needs and Their Families.* Division of Early Childhood Task Force on Recommended Practices. Reston, Va.: Council for Exceptional Children.

Cummins, J. 1998. "Beyond Adversarial Discourse: Searching for Common Ground in the Education of Bilingual Students" (Unpublished manuscript). University of Toronto.

Derman-Sparks, L. 1989. *Anti-Bias Curriculum: Tools for Empowering Young Children.* Washington, D.C.: National Association for the Education of Young Children.

DeVries, R., and B. Zan. 1994. *Moral Classrooms, Moral Children: Creating a Constructivist Atmosphere in Early Education.* New York: Teachers College Press.

Diamond, M., and J. Hopson. 1998. *Magic Trees of the Mind: How to Nurture Your Child's Intelligence, Creativity, and Healthy Emotions from Birth Through Adolescence.* New York: E. P. Dutton.

Dichtelmiller, M. L., and others. 1997. *Work Sampling in the Classroom: A Teacher's Manual.* Ann Arbor, Mich.: Rebus, Inc.

Dickinson, D. K.; L. Cote; and M. W. Smith. 1993. "Learning Vocabulary in Preschool: Social and Discourse Contexts Affecting Vocabulary Growth," in *The Development of Literacy Through Social Interaction,* 67–78. New Directions for Child Development, no. 61: The Jossey-Bass Education Service. Edited by C. Daiute. San Francisco: Jossey Bass.

Dunn, L. M., and L. M. Dunn. 1981. *Peabody Picture Vocabulary Test* (Revised edition). Circle Pines, Minn.: American Guidance Service.

Dutton, W. H.; A. Dutton; and B. Dutton. 1996. *Mathematics Children Use and Understand.* Napa, Calif.: Rattle OK Publications.

Ehri, L. C., and L. S. Wilce. 1980. "The Influence of Orthography of Readers' Conceptualization of the Phonemic Structure of Words," *Applied Psycholinguistics,* 1, 371–85.

Ehri, L. C., and L. S. Wilce. 1985. "Movement into Reading: Is the First Stage of Printed Word Learning Visual or Phonetic?" *Reading Research Quarterly,* 20, 163–79.

Eisenberg, E. 1997. "Meeting Adult Needs Within the Classroom," *Child Care Information Exchange* (September), 53–56.

Epstein, A. 1993. *Training for Quality.* Ypsilanti, Mich.: High/Scope Press.

Epstein, J. L. 1992. "School and Family Partnerships," in *Encyclopedia of Educational Research* (Sixth edition). Edited by M. Alkin. New York: MacMillan.

ERIC/EECE. 1996. *The Project Approach Catalog.* Edited by J. J. Helm. Champaign, Ill.: ERIC Clearinghouse on Elementary and Early Childhood Education.

Evergreen Community School. 1999. Teachers' Documentation of Children's Work. Santa Monica, Calif.: Evergreen Community School.

Feeney, S., and K. Kipnis. 1989. "NAEYC Code of Ethical Conduct and Statement of Commitment," *Young Children,* 45 (1), 24–29.

Frede, E. 1995. "The Role of Program Quality in Producing Early Childhood Program Benefits," *Future of Children,* 5 (3), 115–32.

Fromboluti, C. S., and N. Rinck. 1999. *Early Childhood: Where Learning Begins—Mathematics.* Washington, D.C.: U.S. Department of Education, Office of Educational Research and Improvement.

Fuson, K. C. 1988. *Children's Counting and Concepts of Number.* New York: Springer-Verlag.

Garcia, E. E., and others. 1995. "Meeting the Challenge of Linguistic and Cultural Diversity in Early Childhood Education," in *Yearbook in Early Childhood Education.* Vol. 6. New York: Teachers College Press.

Gardner, H. 1993. *Frames of Mind: The Theory of Multiple Intelligences* (Second edition). New York: Basic Books.

Geary, D. C. 1994. *Children's Mathematical Development.* Washington, D.C.: American Psychological Association.

Gelman, R. 1982. "Accessing One-to-One Correspondence: Still Another Paper About Conservation," *British Journal of Psychology,* Vol. 73, 209–20.

Gelman, R., and C. R. Gallistel. 1978. *The Child's Understanding of Number.* Cambridge, Mass.: Harvard University Press.

Ginsburg, H., and S. Opper. 1988. *Piaget's Theory of Intellectual Development.* Englewood Cliffs, N.J.: Prentice Hall.

Ginsburg, H. P., and R. L. Russell. 1981. "Social Class and Racial Influences on Early Mathematical Thinking," *Monographs of the Society for Research in Child Development,* 46 (6) (Serial no. 193).

Ginsburg, H. P.; A. Klein; and P. Starkey. 1998. "The Development of Children's Mathematical Thinking: Connecting Research with Practice," in *Child Psychology in Practice.* Vol. 4 of *Handbook of Child Psychology* (Fifth edition), 401–76. Edited by W. Damon, I. E. Sigel, and K. A. Renninger. New York: John Wiley.

Goldenberg, C., and R. Gallimore. 1995. "Immigrant Latino Parents' Values and Beliefs About Their Children's Education: Continuities and Discontinuities Across Cultures and Generations," *Advances in Motivation and Achievement,* 9, 183–228.

Greenman, J. 1988. *Caring Spaces, Learning Places: Children's Environments That Work.* Redmond, Wash.: Child Care Information Exchange.

Greeno, J. G.; M. S. Riley; and R. Gelman. 1984. "Conceptual Competence and Children's Counting," *Cognitive Psychology,* 16, 94–143.

Greenspan, S. I., and S. J. Meisels. 1996. "Toward a New Vision for the Developmental Assessment of Infants and Young Children," in *New Visions for the Developmental Assessment of Infants and Young Children,* 11–26. Edited by S. J. Meisels and E. Fenichel. Washington, D.C.: Zero to Three: The National Center for Infants, Toddlers, and Families.

Halverson, L. E. 1971. "The Young Child: The Significance of Motor Development," in *The Significance of the Young Child's Motor Development.* Washington, D.C.: National Association for the Education of Young Children.

Harms, T.; R. M. Clifford; and D. Cryer. 1998. *Early Childhood Environment Rating Scale* (Revised edition). New York: Teachers College Press.

Hartup, W. 1991. "Having Friends, Making Friends, and Keeping Friends: Relationships as Educational Contexts," *ERIC Digest.* Urbana, Ill.: ERIC Clearinghouse on Elementary and Early Childhood Education.

Haugen, K. 1997. *Using Your Senses to Adapt Environments: Checklist for an Accessible Environment.* Redmond, Wash.: Child Care Information Exchange.

Haughland, S. W., and D. D. Shade. 1990. *Developmental Evaluations of Software for Young Children* (1990 edition). New York: Delmar.

Heath, S. B. 1983. *Ways with Words: Language, Life, and Work in Communities and Classrooms.* Cambridge, Mass.: Cambridge University Press.

Hernandez, D. J. 1995. "Changing Demographics: Past and Future Demands for Early Childhood Programs," *The Future of Children* (winter), 5.

Hess, R. D., and S. Holloway. 1984. "Family and School as Educational Institutions," in *Review of Child Development Research.* Vol. 7 of *The Family,* 179–222. Edited by R. D. Parke. Chicago: University of Chicago Press.

High/Scope Educational Research Foundation. 1999. *Child Observation Record.* Ypsilanti, Mich.: High/Scope Press.

Hohmann, C. 1994. "Staff Development Practices for Integrating Technology into Early Childhood Education," in *Young Children: Active Learners in a Technological Age,* 93–104. Edited by J. L. Wright and D. D. Shade. Washington, D.C.: National Association for the Education of Young Children.

Hohmann, M., and D. P. Weikart. 1995. *Educating Young Children: Active Learning Practices for Preschool and Childcare Programs.* Ypsilanti, Mich.: High/Scope Press.

Holloway, S. D., and B. Fuller. 1999. "Families and Child-Care Institutions: Divergent Research and Policy Viewpoints," in *The Silent Crisis in U.S. Child Care: Annals, American Academy of Political and Social Science,* 563, 98–115. Edited by S. Helburn. Thousand Oaks, Calif.: Sage Publications.

Holloway, S. D., and others. 1997. *Through My Own Eyes: Single Mothers and the Cultures of Poverty.* Cambridge, Mass.: Harvard University Press.

Hoover-Dempsey, K. B., and H. M. Sandler. 1997. "Why Do Parents Become Involved in Their Children's Education?" *Review of Educational Research,* 67, 3–42.

Howes, C., and C. E. Hamilton. 1993. "Child Care for Young Children," in *Handbook of Research on the Education of Young Children,* 322–36. Edited by B. Spodek, New York: Macmillan.

Hundert, J., and others. 1998. "A Descriptive Analysis of Developmental and Social Gains of Children with Severe Disabilities in Segregated and Inclusive Preschools in Southern Ontario," *Early Childhood Research Quarterly,* 13, 49–66.

Hyson, M. C.; K. Hirsh-Pasek; and L. Rescorla. 1990. "The Classroom Practices Inventory: An Observation Instrument Based on NAYEC's Guidelines for Developmentally Appropriate Practices for 4- and 5-Year-Old Children," *Early Childhood Research Quarterly,* 5 (4), 475–94.

Jones, E., and J. Nimmo. 1994. *Emergent Curriculum.* Washington, D.C.: National Association for the Education of Young Children.

Jones, E., and G. Reynolds. 1992. *The Play's the Thing: Teachers' Roles in Children's Play.* New York: Teachers College Press.

Kagan, S. L., and M. J. Neuman. 1996. "The Relationship Between Staff Education and Training and Quality in Child Care Programs," *Child Care Information Exchange* (January), 65–70.

Kamii, C., and G. DeClark. 1985. *Young Children Reinvent Arithmetic: Implications of Piaget's Theory.* New York: Teachers College Press.

Katz, L. G. 1993. "Multiple Perspectives on the Quality of Early Childhood Programs," *ERIC Digest.* Champaign, Ill.: ERIC Clearinghouse on Elementary and Early Childhood Education.

Katz, L. G., and S. C. Chard. 1989. *Engaging Children's Minds: The Project Approach.* Norwood, N.J.: Ablex.

Katz, L. G., and S. C. Chard. 1996. "The Contribution of Documentation to the Quality of Early Childhood Education," *ERIC Digest.* Champaign, Ill.: ERIC Clearinghouse on Elementary and Early Childhood Education (April).

Katz, L. G., and D. E. McClellan. 1997. *Fostering Children's Social Competence: The Teacher's Role.* Washington, D.C.: National Association for the Education of Young Children.

Kim, U., and S. Choi. 1994. "Individualism, Collectivism, and Child Development: A Korean Perspective," in *The Cross-Cultural Roots of Minority Child Development,* 227–57. Edited by P. M. Greenfield and R. R. Cocking. Hillsdale, N.J.: Erlbaum.

Kisker, E., and others. 1991. *A Profile of Child Care Settings: Early Education and Care in 1990.* Princeton, N.J.: Mathematica Policy Research, Inc.

Klein, A., and J. Langer. 1991. "The Early Development of Division: Social Sharing or Numerical Distribution?" in *Young Children's Developing Arithmetic Knowledge*. Symposium presented at the meeting of the Jean Piaget Society, Philadelphia, Pa.

Klein, A., and P. Starkey. 2000. *Berkeley Math Readiness Curriculum*. Berkeley, Calif.: PRESS.

Kontos, S., and others. 1994. *Quality in Family Child Care and Relative Care*. New York: Teacher's College Press.

Koplow, L. 1996. "If You're Sad and You Know It," in *Unsmiling Faces: How Preschools Can Heal*. Edited by L. Koplow. New York: Teachers College Press.

Lally, J. R. 1997. "Brain Development in Infancy: A Critical Period," *Bridges*, 3 (1).

Lally, J. R.; P. L. Mangione; and A. Honig. 1988. "The Syracuse University Family Development Research Program: Long-Range Impact of an Early Intervention with Low-Income Children and Their Families," in *Parent Education in Early Childhood Intervention: Emerging Directions in Theory, Research, and Practice*. Edited by D. Powell. Norwood, N.J.: Ablex.

Lamorey, S., and D. D. Bricker. 1993. "Integrated Programs: Effects on Young Children and Their Parents," in *Integrating Young Children with Disabilities into Community-Based Programs: From Research to Implementation*, 249–69. Edited by C. Peck, S. Odom, and D. Bricker. Baltimore: Paul H. Brookes Publishing Co.

Langone, J.; D. M. Malone; and T. Kinsley. 1999. "Technology Solutions for Young Children with Developmental Concerns," *Infants and Young Children* (April), 65–76.

Layzer, J. I.; B. D. Goodson; and M. Moss. 1993. *Life in Preschool: Observational Study of Early Childhood Programs, Final Report*. Vol. 1. Cambridge, Mass.: Abt Associates, Development Assistance Corporation, and RMC Research Corporation.

Lazar, I., and others. 1982. "Lasting Effects of Early Education: A Report from the Consortium for Longitudinal Studies," in *Monographs of the Society for Research in Child Development*, no. 47 (Serial no. 195). Chicago: University of Chicago Press.

Link, G.; M. Beggs; and E. Seiderman. 1997. *Serving Families*. San Francisco: Study Center Press.

Love, J. M.; P. A. Schochet; and A. Meckstrom. 1996. *Are They in Any Real Danger? What Research Does—and Doesn't—Tell Us About Childcare Quality and Children's Well-Being*. Princeton, N.J.: Mathematica Policy Research, Inc.

McDonald, D. T. 1979. *Music in Our Lives*. Washington, D.C.: National Association for the Education of Young Children.

Meisels, S. J. 1994. "Designing Meaningful Measurements for Early Childhood," in *Diversity and Developmentally Appropriate Practices: Challenges for Early Childhood Education*. Edited by B. L. Mallory and R. S. New. New York: Teachers College Press.

National Academy Press. 1990. *Who Cares for America's Children: Child Care Policy for the 1990s*. Edited by S. Hayes, F. Palmer, and M. Zaslow. Washington, D.C.: National Academy Press.

National Association for the Education of Young Children. 1987. *Testing of Young Children: Concerns and Cautions*. Washington, D.C.: National Association for the Education of Young Children.

National Association for the Education of Young Children. 1995. *Reaching Potentials: Transforming Early Childhood Curriculum and Assessment.* Vol. 2. Edited by S. Bredecamp and T. Rosegrant. Washington, D.C.: National Association for the Education of Young Children.

National Association for the Education of Young Children. 1996. "NAEYC Position Statement: Technology and Young Children: Ages Three Through Eight," *Young Children,* 51 (6), 11–16. (This position paper may be found on the Web site for NAEYC: *http:// www.naeyc.org/about/about_index.htm.*)

National Association for the Education of Young Children. 1997. *Developmentally Appropriate Practice in Early Childhood Programs* (Revised edition). Edited by S. Bredecamp and C. Copple. Washington, D.C.: National Association for the Education of Young Children.

National Association for the Education of Young Children. 1998. *NAEYC Code of Ethical Conduct and Statement of Commitment* (Revised 1997). Washington, D.C.: National Association for the Education of Young Children. Brochure. (This position paper may be found in Appendix H of this publication and on the Web site for NAEYC: *http://www.naeyc.org/about/ about_index.htm.*)

National Educational Goals Panel. 1998. *Ready Schools.* A Report of the Goal 1 Ready Schools Resource Group. Washington, D.C.: U.S. Government Printing Office.

National Health/Education Consortium. 1994. "Children's Nutrition and Learning," *ERIC Digest.* Champaign, Ill.: ERIC Clearinghouse on Elementary and Early Childhood Education. (June).

National Research Council. 1998. *Preventing Reading Difficulties in Young Children.* Edited by C. E. Snow, M. S. Burns, and P. Griffin. Washington, D.C.: National Academy Press.

National Research Council. 1999. *Starting Out Right: A Guide to Promoting Children's Reading Success.* Edited by S. M. Burns, P. Griffin, and C. E. Snow. Washington, D.C.: National Academy Press.

Odom, S. L., and K. E. Diamond. 1998. "Inclusion of Young Children with Special Needs in Early Childhood Education: The Research Base," *Early Childhood Research Quarterly,* 13, 3–26.

Paley, V. G. 1986. "On Listening to What Children Say," *Harvard Educational Review,* 56 (2), 122–31.

Peck, C. A.; G. C. Furman; and E. Helmstetter. 1993. "Integrated Early Childhood Programs," in *Integrating Young Children with Disabilities into Community Programs.* Edited by C. Peck, S. Odom, and D. Bricker. Baltimore, Md.: Paul H. Brookes Publishing Co.

Peisner-Feinberg, E. S., and others. 1999. *The Children of the Cost, Quality, and Outcomes Study Go to School. Executive Summary.* Chapel Hill: University of North Carolina, Chapel Hill.

Perfetti, C. A., and others. 1987. "Phonemic Knowledge and Learning to Read Are Reciprocal: A Longitudinal Study of First Grade Children," *Merrill-Palmer Quarterly,* 33, 283–319.

Phillips, D. A.; K. McCartney; and S. Scarr. 1987. "Child-Care Quality and Children's Social Development," *Developmental Psychology,* 23, 537–43.

Piaget, J. 1970. "Piaget's Theory," in *Carmichael's Manual of Child Psychology.* Edited by P. M. Musen. New York: Wiley.

Piaget, J., and A. Szeminska. 1952. *The Child's Conception of Number.* London: Routledge and Kegan Paul.

Pianta, R. 1998. *Enhancing Relationships Between Children and Teachers.* Washington, D.C.: American Psychological Association.

Pica, R. 1996. "Beyond Physical Development: Why Young Children Need to Move," *Young Children* (September), 4–11.

Poulsen, M. K. 1996. "Caregiving Strategies for Building Resilience in Children at Risk," in *Project EXCEPTIONAL: A Guide for Training and Recruiting Child Care Providers to Serve Young Children with Disabilities.* Vol. 1, 139. Edited by A. Kushner, L. Cranor, and L. Brekken. Sacramento: California Department of Education.

Powell, D. R. 1989. *Families and Early Childhood Programs.* Washington, D.C.: National Association for the Education of Young Children.

Powell, D. R. 1994. "Parents, Pluralism, and the NAEYC Statement on Developmentally Appropriate Practice," in *Diversity and Developmentally Appropriate Practices: Challenges for Early Childhood Education,* 166–82. Edited by B. Mallory and R. New. New York: Teachers College Press.

Powell, D. R. 1998. "Reweaving Parents into the Fabric of Early Childhood Programs," *Young Children,* 53, 60–67.

Purcell-Gates, V., and K. L. Dahl. 1991. "Low-SES Children's Success and Failure at Early Literacy Learning in Skills-Based Classrooms," *Journal of Reading Behavior,* 23 (1), 1–34.

Rice, M. L. 1991. "Children with Specific Language Impairment: Toward a Model of Teachability," in *Biological and Behavioral Determinants of Language Development.* Edited by N. Kranegor and others. Hillsdale, N.J.: Lawrence Erlbaum Associates.

Roberts, T., and C. Corbett. 1997. "Efficacy of Explicit English Instruction in Phoneme Awareness and Alphabetic Principle for English Learners and English Proficient Kindergarten Children in Relationship to Oral Language Proficiency, Primary Language, and Verbal Memory." Paper presented at the annual meeting of the National Reading Conference, Scottsdale, Ariz. ERIC, ED 417 403.

Saxe, G. B.; S. R. Guberman; and M. Gearhart. 1987. "Social Processes in Early Number Development," *Monographs of the Society for Research in Child Development,* 52 (2) (Serial no. 126).

Schweinhart, L., and D. Weikart. 1997. *Lasting Differences: The High/Scope Preschool Curriculum Comparison Study Through Age 23.* Ypsilanti, Mich.: High/Scope Press.

Scruggs, T. E., and M. A. Mastropieri. 1996. "Teacher Perceptions of Mainstreaming/Inclusion, 1958–1995: A Research Synthesis," *Exceptional Children,* 63, 59–74.

Shane, R. 1999. "Making Connections: A 'Number Curriculum' for Preschoolers," in *Mathematics in the Early Years.* Edited by Juanita V. Copley. Reston, Va.: National Council of Teachers of English.

Sharpe, C. 1997. *Competencies for the Various Levels of the Child Development Permit.* Pasadena, Calif.: Pacific Oaks College.

Shore, R. 1997. *Rethinking the Brain: New Insights into Early Development.* New York: Families and Work Institute.

Siegler, R. S., and M. Robinson. 1982. "The Development of Numerical Understandings," in *Advances in Child Development and Behavior,* Vol. 15, 241–312. Edited by H. W. Reese and L. P. Lipsitt. New York: Academic Press.

Starkey, P., and A. Klein. 1992. "Economic and Cultural Influences on Early Mathematical Development," in *New Directions in Child and Family Research: Shaping Head Start in the 90s,* 440–443. Edited by F. L. Parker and others.

Starkey, P., and A. Klein. 2000. *Supporting Young Children's Readiness for School Mathematics Through a Prekindergarten Classroom and Family Math Curriculum.* Final report submitted to the National Institute on Early Childhood Development and Education. Washington, D.C.: U.S. Department of Education, Office of Educational Research and Improvement.

Tharp, R. G. 1989. "Psychocultural Variables and Constants: Effects on Teaching and Learning in Schools," special issue on "Children and Their Development: Knowledge Base, Research Agenda, and Social Policy Application," *American Psychologist,* 44 (2), 349–59.

Trister Dodge, D., and L. Colker. 1992. *The Creative Curriculum for Early Childhood* (Third edition). Washington, D.C.: Teaching Strategies, Inc.

University of Colorado. 1995. *Cost, Quality, and Child Outcomes in Child Care Centers.* Edited by S. Helburn. Denver: University of Colorado, Denver, Economics Department.

Valdés, G. 1996. *Con Respeto: Bridging the Distances Between Culturally Diverse Families and Schools.* New York: Teachers College Press.

Vygotsky, L. 1978. *Mind in Society: The Development of Higher Psychological Processes.* Cambridge, Mass.: Harvard University Press.

Wadsworth, B. 1996. *Piaget's Theory of Cognitive and Affective Development.* White Plains, N.Y.: Longman Publishers.

Wagner, S. H., and J. Walters. 1982. "A Longitudinal Analysis of Early Number Concepts: From Number to Number," in *Action and Thought: From Sensorimotor Schemes to Symbolic Operations,* 137–61. Edited by G. E. Forman. New York: Academic Press.

Whitebook, M., and D. Bellm. 1999. *Taking on Turnover: An Action Guide for Child Care Center Teachers and Directors.* Washington, D.C.: Center for the Child Care Workforce.

Whitebook, M., and others. 1996. *California Child Care and Development and Compensation Study: Towards Promising Policy and Practice.* Washington, D.C.: National Center for the Early Childhood Work Force; Palo Alto, Calif.: American Institutes for Research.

Whitebook, M.; C. Howes; and D. Phillips. 1990. *Who Cares? Child Care Teachers and the Quality of Care in America.* Final Report of the National Child Care Staffing Study. Oakland, Calif.: Child Care Employee Project.

Whitehurst, G. J., and C. J. Lonigan. 1998. "Child Development and Emergent Literacy," *Child Development,* 69 (3), 848–72.

Wolery, M. 1994. "Implementing Instruction for Young Children with Special Needs in Early Childhood Classrooms," in *Including Children with Special Needs in Early Childhood Programs.* Edited by M. Wolery and J. S. Wilbers. Washington, D.C.: National Association for the Education of Young Children.

Wolery, M., and J. S. Wilbers. 1994. *Including Children with Special Needs in Early Childhood Programs.* Washington, D.C.: National Association for the Education of Young Children.

Wolery, M.; P. S. Strain; and D. B. Bailey, Jr. 1992. "Reaching Potentials of Children with Special Needs," in *Reaching Potentials: Appropriate Curriculum and Assessment for Young Children,* Vol. 1, 96–97. Edited by S. Bredekamp and T. Rosegrant. Washington, D.C.: National Association for the Education of Young Children.

Wynn, K. 1990. "Children's Understanding of Counting," *Cognition,* 36, 155–93.

Appendixes

Summary of the Guidelines

PROGRAM FOUNDATIONS

Planning the Preschool Environment

1. The environment is safe and comfortable for children and adults.

2. The environment is arranged to maximize learning, facilitate movement, minimize distractions, and organize children's play.

3. The materials in the environment are interesting, engaging, and age appropriate.

4. The environment is supportive of diverse cultures and roles.

5. The environment welcomes parents and provides a place for communication between staff and parents.

6. The environment is accessible to children with disabilities or other special needs.

7. The environment makes appropriate use of technology.

Addressing Cultural Diversity

1. The program encourages and supports appreciation of and respect for individual and group similarities and differences, making the acceptance of diversity a theme that is central to the classroom climate.

2. Program materials reflect the characteristics, values, and practices of diverse cultural groups.

3. Whenever reasonable, teachers engage in practices that are consistent with those from children's homes.

4. Teachers attempt, as much as possible, to learn about the history, beliefs, and practices of the children and families they serve, and they receive support for their efforts from the early care and education center.

5. Children are encouraged to recognize and develop strategies to use when they encounter social injustice, bias, and prejudice.

Planning for Assessment

1. Assessment is done to benefit the children and to enhance the effectiveness of parents and teachers.

2. Assessment includes multiple sources of information and is balanced across the cognitive, social, emotional, and health domains.

3. Assessment takes place in a context or setting that is natural, nonthreatening, and familiar to the children.

4. Assessment is continuous and is used regularly for planning and developing specific strategies to support children's learning and development.

5. Assessment for admission or placement purposes has few appropriate uses in preschool; but, if it is done, it should have an established reliability and validity, and it should be conducted by trained examiners.

6. Programs direct significant efforts toward developing assessments that are accurate, fair, and free of cultural bias.

7. As much as possible, parents are aware of and involved in assessments of their children.

Including Children with Disabilities or Other Special Needs

1. Teachers accept and actively support the concept of inclusion by creating a classroom environment in which all children and families feel that they are welcome.

2. Teachers are a part of the educational team that develops and implements individualized education programs (IEPs) for children eligible to receive special education services.

3. Teachers work collaboratively with other specialists to determine appropriate modifications in the curriculum, instructional methods, or classroom environment.

4. Programs provide sufficient release time, training, information, and support for teachers to plan and consult regarding children with disabilities or other special needs.

5. Teachers work closely with families in an educational partnership and provide them with appropriate information and support.

Involving Parents and Families

1. The teacher incorporates parents' goals into program instruction and supports the involvement of parents in helping their children to attain those goals.

2. The program creates an environment where parents feel empowered and comfortable in advocating for their children.

3. The program regularly provides parents with information about activities in the program and about their children's learning and development.

4. The teacher recognizes the role that various family members other than parents may play in promoting children's development.

5. The program supports and is an advocate for strong families.

Organizing Staff Preparation and Development Programs

1. The program has a comprehensive staff development plan.

2. The program provides adequate paid time for professional development activities.

3. The program promotes professionalism and ethical behavior.

4. The program provides opportunities for all staff to participate in decision making.

5. The program provides tools and materials needed by the staff members to advance their professional skills and knowledge.

6. The program employs staff who meet the requirements for education and experience for their positions and encourages advancement along a planned career pathway.

7. The program has a compensation schedule that acknowledges and validates the required training and experience of each staff member.

8. Professional development activities stress the development of cultural competence.

9. The program supports professional development activities that focus on family involvement.

10. The staff development plan incorporates a clearly defined approach to integrating technology in the early childhood education program.

Curriculum

Social and Emotional Development

1. The staff is responsive to children's emotional needs.

2. The program climate, organization, and routine create a sense of safety, security, and predictability.

3. Each child is supported to develop a sense of self-worth and capability.

4. Each child is supported to develop a sense of self as a valued and responsible member of the group.

5. Children are guided and supported to form and maintain satisfying relationships with others.

6. Children are guided and supported to express their emotions in socially acceptable ways.

7. Children's social and cultural backgrounds are taken into account in interpreting their preferences and behaviors in the preschool setting.

8. Children's social behavior is guided in the context of daily activities.

9. The goal of discipline is to promote greater social and emotional competence.

Language and Literacy Development

1. Programs support learning and development in both language and literacy.

2. Programs provide a language-rich and print-rich environment to support children's language and literacy learning across curricular areas.

3. Adults model language and literacy practices as a means to enhance children's learning and development in those areas.

4. Programs implement a language arts curriculum that lays the foundation for children's success in language arts in elementary school.

5. The program recognizes and includes the home languages of English learners.

6. Children's language and literacy development is supported through interaction between preschool staff and the children's families.

Mathematics Learning and Development

1. The program develops and builds on children's existing informal mathematical knowledge, recognizing that children enter preschool with different experiences in mathematics.

2. Teacher-guided and child-initiated activities are integrated in a mathematically rich learning environment, using multiple instructional approaches.

3. The program implements a mathematics curriculum that lays the foundation for children's success in mathematics in elementary school.

4. The program identifies clear, age-appropriate goals for mathematics learning and development.

5. The program establishes a partnership with parents and other caregivers in preparing children for mathematics learning.

Physical and Motor Development

1. The curriculum gives attention to all areas of motor skill development, including gross motor, fine motor, oral motor, and sensorimotor.

2. Consideration is given to children's varying rates of development and acquisition of skills.

3. The program provides many opportunities for free play.

4. Teachers consider children's special health and physical needs when designing physical activities.

Other Curriculum Content Areas

1. The teacher builds on the natural curiosity that children have about the world around them by creating opportunities for exploration of social studies, science, the arts, and health and nutrition. These subjects are part of the program's daily routines and are fully integrated into the program.

   Where appropriate, the program links these content areas with other content areas, such as social–emotional development, language and literacy development, mathematics, and physical and motor development.

Appendix B

Desired Results for Children and Families

"Desired Results for Children and Families," a forthcoming publication of the California Department of Education (CDE), measures how well children and families are doing in meeting the following six broad desired results:

1. Children are personally and socially competent.

2. Children are effective learners.

3. Children show physical and motor competencies.

4. Children are safe and healthy.

5. Families support their children's learning and development.

6. Families achieve their goals.

To assess the extent to which these desired results for children and families have been achieved requires a definition of *indicators, measures,* and *criteria for success.* An *indicator* defines a desired result more specifically so that it can be measured. For example, an indicator of the desired result "Children are personally and socially competent" is "Children show self-awareness and a positive self-concept." Desired results are generally better measured through the use of multiple indicators, no one of which gives full information on all aspects of achievement. A *measure* quantifies the achievement of a particular indicator. For example, a measure for the indicator given previously might be a four-year-old who "identifies himself or herself as a part of a family or social group" or "demonstrates confidence in his or her own abilities." The *criterion for success* is that children show individual progress toward achieving the age-appropriate and developmentally appropriate measures for each indicator that defines the desired result.

Achievement of the four desired results for children will be measured through the use of the Desired Results Developmental Profile tool, and achievement of the two desired results for families will be measured through the distribution of a family survey. Programs will be responsible for collecting desired results data, implementing new program standards, conducting a yearly self-assessment, and participating in a periodic state-led coordinated compliance review (CCR).

Note: More information on Desired Results may be found at the following Web site: *http://www.cde.ca.gov/cyfsbranch/ child_development/DR2.htm.*

Components of the system will be integrated to support the achievement of the six desired results. The "Desired Results Handbook" will provide an overview of the components and include the tools and instructions for their use. "Desired Results for Children and Families" will measure how well the six desired results are being met. The major components found in this publication appear next.

Program Performance Standards

The Desired Results Program Performance Standards will be the requirements for funding of center-based programs and family child care home networks under contract with the CDE/CDD. The standards support the achievement of desired results for children from birth through fourteen years old and their families. All CDE-subsidized programs will be held accountable for meeting these program requirements. Each standard is accompanied by "Guidance," or examples for implementation, and measures for assessing whether the standard has been appropriately implemented. The program standards include those related to compliance with the state's "Funding Terms and Conditions" and those related to program quality.

The standards will be included in a document titled "Desired Results Program Performance Standards for Center-Based Programs and Family Child Care Home Networks." Key dimensions include the standards; assessment and accountability; teaching and learning; opportunity (equal educational access); staffing and professional growth; parent and community involvement; and governance and administration.

Measurement of the implementation of program standards related to "teaching and learning" will be accomplished through the use of standardized environmental rating scales for annual program self-assessment and periodic state validation team reviews.[1]

Developmental Profile

The "Desired Results Developmental Profile" (DRDP) will be an observation tool for recording the achievement of desired results for children. It will be used by child care and development teachers to track and report on children's individual progress. All child care and development programs supported by the CDE will be required to complete developmental profiles twice each year for every preschool child (who attends the program from 6 a.m. to 8 p.m. for a minimum of ten hours per week). The measures that will be included in the developmental profile correspond to each of the four desired results for children. Cognitive, social–emotional, language, and physical developmental domains are interrelated and woven throughout the four desired results.

Measures are grouped into *themes* (e.g., "self-awareness," "healthy habits," "number concepts") which describe the aspect that is being measured for each indicator. The primary source of information for completing the developmental profile should be caregivers' observations of the child during typical daily activities in the early care and education setting. In addition, specific suggestions for teachers to support optimal performance for children with disabilities being assessed with the DRDP will be included in "Tools for Assessors," being developed by the Special Education Division, California Department of Education, which will accompany the Desired Results system. Results from the "Developmental Profile" regarding the child's developmental progress are to be shared with parents during parent conferences or at other meetings. An optional child summary report will accompany the "Developmental Profile."

---

[1]See "Program Quality Standards," in Part 3, "Resources," for more information.

Family Survey

The family survey is designed to gather information related to the two desired results for families and to evaluate families' satisfaction and experiences with center-based and family child care programs. The survey asks for feedback from parents on the child care services that they are receiving. Questions focus on how well child care services are helping to support children's learning and development and on how well the child care services are meeting the needs of the family. Parents are also asked about their satisfaction with various characteristics of the child care program or provider, the types of information that have been provided by the child care program or provider, and changes in the child's primary caregiver.

Program Review Process

All programs subsidized by CDE will be held accountable for implementing the program performance standards that support the achievement of desired results. The program review process includes an annual self-study, a coordinated compliance or contract monitoring review conducted by CDE every four years, and targeted technical assistance to support the best practices leading to the achievement of desired results. Standardized child care and development environmental rating scales and a program review instrument that measures program quality and compliance with program requirements help programs to assess the extent to which they have implemented the standards that support the achievement of desired results.

California Department of Education Initiatives

Desired Results System
Desired Results Matrix for Children and Families
Desired Results Program Standards (in draft)

Function: Evaluation
Level: Policy
Implementation: "Programs for children birth through age fourteen will achieve desired results . . ."

	Classroom	Child	Family
Level: Program	Environmental Rating Scales	Desired Results Child Development Profile	Desired Results Family Survey
Tool: Coordinated Compliance Review Instrument (CCR)			
Implementation: "A high-quality program includes . . ."	"Children have the opportunity to . . ."	"Children are able to . . ."	"Families are able to . . ."

Resources

Birth Through Age Three	Ages Three Through Five	Birth Through Age Six	Ages Four Through Eight	Ages Five Through Fourteen
Program for Infant/Toddler Caregivers **Function:** Training **Level:** Program **Impl.:** "A high-quality program includes . . ." **Function:** Program delivery **Level:** Classroom **Impl.:** "Children have the opportunity to learn . . ."	*Universal Preschool* **Function:** Vision **Level:** Statewide **Impl.:** "All children will have access to . . ." *Prekindergarten Learning and Development Guidelines* **Function:** Program design **Level:** Program **Impl.:** "A high-quality program includes . . ."	*Project EXCEPTIONAL: A Guide . . . to Serve Young Children with Disabilities* **Function:** Program delivery **Level:** Classroom **Impl.:** "Children have the opportunity to learn . . ." *Fostering the Development of a First and a Second Language* **Function:** Program delivery **Level:** Classroom **Impl.:** "Children have the opportunity to learn . . ."	*First Class: A Guide for Early Primary Education* **Function:** Program delivery **Level:** Classroom **Impl.:** "Children have the opportunity to learn . . ."	*Kid's Time: A School-Age Care Program Guide* **Function:** Training **Level:** Program **Impl.:** "A high-quality program includes . . ." **Function:** Program delivery **Level:** Classroom **Impl.:** "Children have the opportunity to learn . . ."

Continuum of Teaching Behaviors

Nondirective	Mediating						Directive
Acknowledge	Model	Facilitate	Support	Scaffold	Co-construct	Demonstrate	Direct
Give attention and positive encouragement to keep a child engaged in an activity.	Display for children a skill or desirable way of behaving in the classroom, through actions only or with cues, prompts, or other forms of coaching.	Offer short-term assistance to help a child achieve the next level of functioning (as an adult does in holding the back of a bicycle while a child pedals).	Provide a fixed form of assistance, such as a bicycle's training wheels, to help a child achieve the next level of functioning.	Set up challenges or assist children to work "on the edge" of their current competence.	Learn or work collaboratively with children on a problem or task, such as building a model or block structure.	Actively display a behavior or engage in an activity while children observe the outcome.	Provide specific directions for children's behavior with narrowly defined dimensions of error.

Source: Reaching Potentials: Transforming Early Childhood Curriculum and Assessment, Vol. 2. Edited by Sue Bredekamp and Teresa Rosegrant. Washington, D.C.: National Association for the Education of Young Children, 1995, p. 21. Reprinted with permission from the National Association for the Education of Young Children.

APPENDIX E

Effective Observation Strategies

The Desired Results system involves direct observation of children, using an instrument called the "Desired Results Developmental Profile" (DRDP). Developmental assessment is designed to deepen understanding of a child's strengths and to identify areas where a child may need additional support. Teachers and other child development professionals are encouraged to complete the developmental profiles through observation, a method of gathering information by carefully and systematically observing children in their early care and education environments.

Conducting Effective Observations

The process of systematically observing the development of children in the context of day-to-day family and early care and education activities is the initial step in finding and planning appropriate strategies to support the continuing development of children and families. Information gathered through observations can help child care providers in arranging the environment and in developing curricular plans and materials.

There are a variety of ways of gathering information through observations, including the following: videotapes and cassette recordings; photographs; portfolios; anecdotal records, diaries, and logs; activity lists; time sampling and event recording; and checklists and rating scales.

Effective observation of children requires training and practice on the part of observers. It also requires an environment that is conducive to documenting children's activities and interactions with minimal effort or interruption to the natural flow of typical daily routines.

Using Observation

When using observation to complete the "Desired Results Developmental Profile" (DRDP), educators need to consider the following points:

1. Use skilled observers.

Observation is a complex, critical skill that can be developed through systematic training and practice. Observers completing the DRDP must be the teacher or caregiver who is the most familiar with the child.

Observers must also do the following:

- Be familiar with the tools, measures, and indicators for the developmental levels being observed.
- Have an in-depth understanding of child development, including cultural variations expressed in children's behavior.
- Identify high-risk behavior or danger signals that may indicate possible disabilities or other detrimental circumstances.
- Understand the child's cultural context. Family and community cultures influence the child's access to multiple approaches to literacy and are also related to expectations regarding a child's educational accomplishments.
- Consider the child's experience. Is the child challenged by premature birth, a medical condition, or poverty? Is the child the product of a healthy, full-term delivery and living in an economically secure and supportive household that affords ample opportunities for play and discovery?
- Be aware of how performance styles, motivational factors, and environmental variables influence the judgments made about children's strengths and weaknesses.
- Refrain from labeling and avoid the tendency to place stereotypical expectations on children.
- Be aware of a child's total performance (across developmental domains), even when you are focusing on a single aspect of behavior.

2. Set up the environment to support effective observations of children.

Observers can do the following to provide an appropriate environment:

- Arrange activities so that the observers can watch from a place where they can hear children's conversations.
- Plan activities that do not require the full assistance of teachers or caregivers when they wish to observe a child.
- Seat the observer unobtrusively near children's activities.
- Scatter "observation chairs" at strategic locations throughout the program, if possible. Children who are accustomed to having observers present who are "writing" are more likely to behave naturally and allow the observer to take notes without interruption.
- Carry a small notepad in a pocket. In several places on the wall, hang clipboards with lined paper and an attached pencil.

3. Keep a few specific points in mind.

Observers can do the following to improve their effectiveness:

- Focus on observing exactly what the child does. Be as objective as possible. Do not let prior opinions or stereotypes influence your judgment.
- Record your observations as soon as possible. Details may be important and can be easily forgotten.
- Observe in a variety of settings and at different times during the day.

- Be realistic in scheduling observations. Haphazard or incomplete observations will not present an accurate or comprehensive picture of the child's behavior.
- Focus on one child at a time. Assign staff to observe specific children so that those observers can concentrate on getting to know a few children very well.
- Observe children during their natural daily routines. Avoid being obvious.
- Ensure confidentiality at all times.
- Plan ahead. Are there times when the availability of extra staff or the nature of the day's activities seems better suited to observation?

APPENDIX F

Special Needs Legislation and Services

This appendix contains information on federal legislation and services for children with disabilities. Those services cover criteria for determining children's eligibility for special education and for selecting the most appropriate educational setting for children with special needs.

Americans with Disabilities Act

The Americans with Disabilities Act (ADA) of 1990, a landmark civil rights protection bill, guarantees equal opportunities in employment, public accommodations, transportation, and state and local governmental services. Under the ADA, child care providers are required to make reasonable accommodations to serve persons who meet the definition of *disabled* and allow them the opportunity to participate in or benefit from services offered. Providers of programs must understand the provisions under the ADA.

"The ADA's protection applies primarily, but not exclusively, to *disabled* individuals. An individual is *disabled* if he or she meets at least any one of the following tests:[1]

1. He or she has a physical or mental impairment that substantially limits one or more of his or her major life activities.

2. He or she has a record of such an impairment.

3. He or she is regarded as having such an impairment."

Resources are available that help in determining admissibility to care and reasonable accommodations. (See the Web site: *http://janweb.icdi.wvu.edu/kinder/overview.htm*.)

Individuals with Disabilities Education Act

The 1997 amendments to the Individuals with Disabilities Education Act (IDEA) were enacted into Public Law 105-17 to redirect its focus on improving results for children with disabilities. Implicit in the law is the concept of inclusion. Several of the key provisions to be found in IDEA 1997 promote the following:

1. Individualized education programs (IEPs) that focus on improving results through participation in the general curriculum:

---

[1]This material appears on the Web site: *http://janweb.icdi.wvu.edu/kinder/overview.htm*.

a. Participation of regular education teachers in the IEP

b. Inclusion in the IEP of specific special education, related services, supplementary aids and services, and program modifications or supports for school personnel

2. Education of disabled children together with nondisabled children

a. Relating a child's education to that which nondisabled children are receiving

b. Providing a statement of the extent to which a child will not participate with nondisabled children in the regular class

3. Strengthening the role of parents and the fostering of partnerships between parents and schools

a. Ensuring that parents have the opportunity to participate in meetings for identification, evaluation, and the educational placement or provision of a free appropriate public education

b. Offering parents mediation as a voluntary option whenever a hearing is requested

Additional information about parents' and families' rights with regard to special education appears in *Special Education Rights of Parents and Children Under the Individuals with Disabilities Education Act, Part B* (California Department of Education 2000c).

Services for Children with Disabilities

During the 1999–2000 school year, 58,491 children aged three through five were enrolled in special education programs in California.[1] Section 8208 of the California *Education Code* outlines the qualifications for eligibility for special education, the rights of children and parents, and the guidelines for developing and implementing an individualized education program for each child.

Eligibility for Special Education

To qualify for special education services, children three through five years of age must meet *one* of the following criteria:

1. The child has a *significant* delay in *one* of the following areas: gross or fine motor development, receptive or expressive language development, social or emotional development, cognitive development, or visual development.

2. The child has a *moderate delay* in any of the *two* areas listed in item 1.

3. The child has a disabling condition or an established medical disability that can include:

- Autism
- Deaf-blindness
- Deafness
- Hearing impairment
- Mental retardation
- Multiple disabilities
- Orthopedic impairment

---

[1] "Special Needs Student Data Report," December 1999. (For more information on this report, contact the Special Education Division, California Department of Education.)

- Other health impairment
- Serious emotional disturbance
- Specific learning disability
- Speech or language impairment in one or more area: voice, fluency, language, and articulation
- Traumatic brain injury

Children are not eligible for special education and services if they do not otherwise meet the eligibility criteria and their educational needs are due primarily to:

- Unfamiliarity with the English language
- Temporary physical disabilities
- Social maladjustment
- Environmental, cultural, or economic factors

THE GOALS OF CALIFORNIA'S SPECIAL EDUCATION PROGRAMS

California *Education Code* Section 56441 lists the following goals for California's special education programs:

- Reduce significantly the potential impact of any disabling conditions.
- Produce substantial gains in the development of physical, cognitive, language and speech, psychosocial, and self-help skills.
- Help to prevent the development of secondary disabling conditions.
- Reduce family stresses.
- Reduce societal dependency and institutionalization.
- Reduce the need for special class placement in special education programs once the children reach school age.
- Save substantial costs to society and schools.

Appropriate Educational Setting

California's *Education Code* requires teachers, to the greatest extent possible, to educate children with identified disabilities in regular classrooms and with typically developing children. This requirement includes providing children with access to the same general curriculum and activities in such settings as public and private preschools, Head Start programs, and center-based or home-based child care programs. When full participation in a regular classroom and curriculum does not best serve a disabled child's needs, the child's individualized education program may specify pull-out services, special day class programs, or part-time participation in early care and education programs. Services for children with disabilities and their families may include:

- Providing early childhood special education services in the least restrictive environment or in those settings typical for young children

- Supporting children's development in the least restrictive environment that offers opportunities for play, social–emotional development, and preacademic skills

- Providing recommendations and assistance in accessing equipment and specialized materials appropriate for children's levels of development

- Observing and monitoring the child's growth and development across a variety of settings and activities

- Interacting and consulting with family members, regular preschool teachers, and other service providers to best meet the child's needs

- Assisting parents in accessing and coordinating services provided by other agencies or programs in the community

- Providing appropriate related services that include counseling and training for parents to help them understand and meet their child's unique strengths and needs

- Ensuring that instructional adult-to-child ratios for children served in group settings shall be one to five or less, depending on the individual needs of the child (California *Education Code* Section 56441.5)

The Map to Services for Children with Special Needs and Their Families

Many families and child care providers have questions about children's development. Although many resources are available to both families and providers, trying to navigate and understand the system for delivering services can be confusing and overwhelming. Both legal and practical information is provided to help you. This chart has been developed and reviewed by parents, providers, and professionals to help other parents understand the system for delivering services to children with special needs. Please call the California Child Care Healthline at 800-333-3212 if you have questions or comments about the information or have a concern about your child.

AGE	QUESTIONS OR CONCERNS	REFERRAL	EVALUATION AND ASSESSMENT
Birth to 3	Child appears to have difficulty relating to caregiver or does not meet typical developmental milestones or demonstrate age-appropriate behavior. Providers can: • Observe the child and provide developmental information to the parent. • Share information regarding the child's interests, interactions, and behaviors at home and in the child care setting. • Work closely with families to identify specific areas of concern. • Refer to medical provider to rule out any physical causes, including vision and hearing problems. • Discuss with the family the option to refer their child to the California Early Start Program. Call the Babyline at 800-515-BABY for information and referral sources. • Call the California Child Care Healthline at 800-333-3212 for more information.	Children from birth to three years may qualify for early intervention services in the Early Start Program. The parents may refer their child directly to an Early Start Program or have their health care provider or other professional make the referral. Parents *do not* have to make that first call. After the referral, the parents will be contacted, informed of their rights as parents under the law, and asked whether they wish to initiate services. A service coordinator will be assigned to assist the family. Parents have the right to an evaluation of their child's performance. Referrals should be made to the local regional center or school district. Call the Department of Developmental Services at 800-515-2229 to obtain the phone numbers in your area.	Evaluation may determine whether the child has a delay or disability; identify the child's strengths and concerns about development; and help in planning for intervention. Children referred to the Early Start Program are evaluated by means that are not racially or culturally discriminatory. Evaluation is conducted in the following developmental areas: physical (includes vision, hearing, and health status), cognitive development, communication development, social or emotional development, and adaptive skills. Evaluation and assessment: • Are conducted by a multidisciplinary team of qualified personnel that consist of a nurse, psychologist, educator, or therapists. • Identify the infant or toddler's unique strengths and needs. • With family consent, identify their resources, priorities, and concerns in the language of the parents' choice. • Must be completed within 45 days of referral. • Should be ongoing as child develops and grows.
3 to 5	Child is having difficulty at home or in child care and is not developing as are other children of the same age. Child care providers can: Use the brochure *Early Warning Signs* as a guide. Concerns for preschool children may include the following: • Has limited understanding and use of language • Does not play with other children • Has *very* short attention span • Overly aggressive or frequently hurts self or others • Frequently falls, is clumsy, has poor motor coordination Discuss parents' perception of child's strengths and any concerns. Have parents observe their child in the child care program. Maintain open and ongoing communication with the family and school.	Parents should call the local school district or county office of education to make a referral. Other agencies and child care programs may contact the schools, but *only* with written consent of the family. • The family should contact the regional center (call 800-515-BABY for the local contact) if a developmental disability is suspected. Regional centers have 15 working days to complete the intake process. • A referral to the health care provider should be made to rule out physical or health causes.	School districts evaluate children to determine whether they qualify for special education and related services. Written parent permission is required for the evaluation. Health care and other professionals should stay informed and involved. Information from child care staff may be included as part of the assessment. Assessment: • Must be done in the primary language of the child by a team of professionals. • May be conducted in group care settings, including child care. • Should be unbiased. • Should be completed in all areas of the suspected disability. Parents have the right to request an assessment of their child for eligibility with the regional center if a disability is present. There are legal timelines to the process. For information regarding all parental rights and entitled services in the regional center system, call Protection & Advocacy, Inc., at 800-776-5746.
5 and Older	School-age children are typically identified because of behavior or academic problems in school, such as the following: • Not doing well in school, even after accommodations are made and educational support is provided in the regular classroom • Does not complete or forgets to turn in homework *frequently* • Has learning or behavior problems • Not reading by second grade Child care providers can: • Support families - listen and share what works. • Identify key areas that may be cause for concern. • Maintain open and ongoing communication with the family and school. For older elementary and middle school children: • Problems may occur as children enter a new school or change classes. • Social problems may give parents and providers cause for concern beyond the typical entry into adolescence. • Child care for children with special needs is more difficult to obtain because typical children of this age are often not in group care settings.	Parents may contact the special education department in their local school or district office to make a referral. If a child has a developmental disability, parents should also contact the local regional center. Child care providers may obtain written consent from the family to allow communication between the child care program and the school district to coordinate referral and possible services.	Schools evaluate children with written consent of the parent. Assessment: • Can identify differences between the child's ability and how well s/he is doing in school. • Identify social problems. Student study teams (SSTs) are available at most schools to observe and assess children. SSTs are not required to follow any timelines or provide due process rights for parents, unlike special education. Parents may bypass the SST and make a referral directly to special education. The law requires a *functional behavioral assessment* by mental health professionals for children with *severe* behaviors. The assessment must be conducted before a child is suspended or expelled from school.

ELIGIBILITY	PROGRAM PLANNING	SERVICES	TRANSITION OR PERIODIC REVIEW
Eligibility for services is based on the results of the evaluation and includes one or more of the following conditions: 1. Significant delays in one or more of the following developmental areas: cognitive; physical and motor, including vision and hearing; communication; social or emotional; or adaptive (self-help). 2. "Established risk conditions" means having a high probability of leading to developmental delay (e.g., Down syndrome). 3. High risk of having a developmental disability due to a combination of biomedical risk factors (e.g., low birth weight, prematurity, or medical complications). For children who do *not* qualify for services, a meeting is held to discuss the evaluation results. Families and providers can request specific suggestions for working with the child. The child care provider may attend the meeting if the parent so requests.	Individualized family service plans (IFSPs) are developed for infants and toddlers who qualify for the Early Start Program and include the following information: • Child's present level of development • If the family consents, the resources, priorities, and concerns of the family • Major outcomes desired for the child/family • Specific early intervention and other appropriate services necessary • Dates for initiation and duration of services • Name of the service coordinator responsible for implementation and coordination with other agencies and persons • Planning for the child's transition at age 3 to a preschool program or other community services • Informed written consent of parents or guardian Child care providers may attend IFSP meetings if the parent requests their presence. The IFSP meeting is conducted in the language of the family or through the use of interpreters.	A variety of services may be offered to promote the child's development and support the family. Services are provided in *natural environments*, such as: • The child's home • The child care center and/or family child care homes • Other settings where there are typically developing children	The IFSP must be reviewed every 6 months or as needed or requested. The Early Start Program ends when the child turns 3. A transition plan to preschool is written as part of the IFSP when the child is 2 years, 9 months (or earlier if needed) to prepare for the change in program. The service coordinator facilitates the transition and the exchange of information between regional centers, schools, and other agencies. Transition steps may include: • Obtaining parental consent for a referral to the school district for special education services • Obtaining parental consent for referrals to other community agencies • Arrangements for evaluations to determine eligibility for special education services at age 3 • Developing an individualized education program (IEP) to be implemented by age 3 At the request of parents, child care providers may give recommendations for the transition process, information to preschool programs, and support to families.
To qualify for special education services, children 3 to 5 years of age must meet one of the following criteria: 1. The child has a *significant delay* in one of the following skill areas: gross or fine motor development, receptive or expressive language, social or emotional development, cognitive development, or visual development. 2. The child has a *moderate delay* in any *two* areas above. 3. The child has a disabling condition or established medical disability that can include autism, deaf-blindness, deafness, hearing impairment, mental retardation, multiple disabilities, orthopedic impairment, other health impairment, serious emotional disturbance, specific learning disability, speech or language impairment, traumatic brain injury, or visual impairment.	Individualized education programs (IEPs) are developed for children who qualify for special education and contain the following information: • Present levels of educational performance • Measurable annual goals and short-term objectives • Services related to special education • Supplementary aids and services and program modifications or supports provided for school personnel • Explanation of why child will *not* participate in the regular class • Individual modifications needed to participate in state and districtwide assessments • Projected dates to begin services, the frequency, location, and duration; dates of modifications • How child's progress is measured and how parents will be regularly informed School districts develop a "504 Plan" for children with a disability who require adaptation or services but do not qualify for special education. This can be used for children with health problems (e.g., asthma, diabetes, seizures) and attention deficit disorder. Regional centers develop an individualized program plan (IPP) for children who qualify for their services.	Services are provided in the least restrictive environment as decided by the IEP team, which may include the home, preschool, or child care setting . . . Regional center services are based on the child/family needs as identified on the IPP. Child care providers may invite special education and other specialist staff to observe the child in your program, show you what to do, and give you information on how to best improve the child's skills and meet his/her needs. The specialists can also learn by seeing the child in a "typical" setting with "typical" children.	An appropriate reassessment should be conducted before the child enters kindergarten to determine whether s/he still needs special education and to plan for the appropriate services and supports. Families should visit sites and determine the best program based on the child's strengths and family concerns. Child care providers help families by: • Providing support, • Preparing the child/family for change, • Accompanying the parent on site visits, and • Talking with staff of special education and other programs regarding the child's strengths and needs.
Children qualify for special education services under the following categories: Hearing impairment Visual impairment Language or speech disorder • very difficult to understand • abnormal voice • fluency disorder (stuttering) • language disorder (speaking or understanding) Severe orthopedic impairment Other health impairments (chronic or acute health problems) Autistic-like behaviors Mental retardation Emotional disturbance Specific learning disabilities Traumatic brain injury If the child has a developmental disability, s/he continues to be eligible for services at the regional center.	Child care providers can: • Get parents' permission to share relevant information about the child between the service providers and the child care staff. • Request assistance and communicate with specialists to get information about children to plan better and support them. • Ask for help by inviting the special education staff to visit the child care program and offer recommendations. • Participate as part of the team to develop and implement the IEP. Specialized programs and vocational and recreational services are available in communities. Some programs provide services before and after school. Contact the local parks and recreation programs, Special Olympics, or AYSO (American Youth Soccer Organization).	Since most children of this age are in school, special education services are typically provided in school during school hours. • Children may be bused to other service providers (e.g., CCS-Medical Therapy Units for occupational and/or physical therapy). • Services must be provided in the *least restrictive environment* (e.g., school, home, or private school). Special education consultation or services are allowed to be provided in a child care setting. Regional center services continue for children who remain eligible.	As children in special education go from one service to another or one class to another (e.g., from speech therapy to resource room or learning center or to a special day class), they make transitions. For older children with special needs, transition to high school may be difficult; children and families need much support at this time. Beginning at age 14, each child with a disability must have a transition plan in the IEP.

*From: California Department of Education. 1999. "The Map to Services for Children with Special Needs and Their Families." *Bridges,* 4 (1), 20–21.

APPENDIX H

NAEYC Code of Ethical Conduct and Statement of Commitment

NAEYC Position Statement

Adopted 1989
Amended 1997

Code of Ethical Conduct

Preamble

NAEYC recognizes that many daily decisions required of those who work with young children are of a moral and ethical nature. The NAEYC Code of Ethical Conduct offers guidelines for responsible behavior and sets forth a common basis for resolving the principal ethical dilemmas encountered in early childhood care and education. The primary focus is on daily practice with children and their families in programs for children from birth through 8 years of age, such as infant/toddler programs, preschools, child care centers, family child care homes, kindergartens, and primary classrooms. Many of the provisions also apply to specialists who do not work directly with children, including program administrators, parent and vocational educators, college professors, and child care licensing specialists.

Core Values

Standards of ethical behavior in early childhood care and education are based on commitment to core values that are deeply rooted in the history of our field. We have committed ourselves to:

- ◆ Appreciating childhood as a unique and valuable stage of the human life cycle

- ◆ Basing our work with children on knowledge of child development

- ◆ Appreciating and supporting the close ties between the child and family

- ◆ Recognizing that children are best understood and supported in the context of family, culture, community, and society

National Association for the Education of Young Children. 1998. *NAEYC Code of Ethical Conduct and Statement of Commitment* (Revised 1997). Washington, D.C.: National Association for the Education of Young Children. Brochure. ©1998 National Association for the Education of Young Children. Reprinted by permission of the publisher. Updated February 6, 1998.

- Respecting the dignity, worth, and uniqueness of each individual (child, family member, and colleague)

- Helping children and adults achieve their full potential in the context of relationships that are based on trust, respect, and positive regard

Conceptual Framework

The Code sets forth a conception of our professional responsibilities in four sections, each addressing an arena of professional relationships: (1) children, (2) families, (3) colleagues, and (4) community and society. Each section includes an introduction to the primary responsibilities of the early childhood practitioner in that arena, a set of ideals pointing in the direction of exemplary professional practice, and a set of principles defining practices that are required, prohibited, and permitted.

The ideals reflect the aspirations of practitioners. **The principles** are intended to guide conduct and assist practitioners in resolving ethical dilemmas encountered in the field. There is not necessarily a corresponding principle for each ideal. Both ideals and principles are intended to direct practitioners to those questions which, when responsibly answered, will provide the basis for conscientious decision making. While the Code provides specific direction and suggestions for addressing some ethical dilemmas, many others will require the practitioner to combine the guidance of the Code with sound professional judgment.

The ideals and principles in this Code present a shared conception of professional responsibility that affirms our commitment to the core values of our field. The Code publicly acknowledges the responsibilities that we in the field have assumed and in so doing supports ethical behavior in our work. Practitioners who face ethical dilemmas are urged to seek guidance in the applicable parts of this Code and in the spirit that informs the whole.

Ethical Dilemmas Always Exist

Often, "the right answer"—the best ethical course of action to take?—is not obvious. There may be no readily apparent, positive way to handle a situation. One important value may contradict another. When we are caught "on the horns of a dilemma," it is our professional responsibility to consult with all relevant parties in seeking the most ethical course of action to take.

Section I: Ethical Responsibilities to Children

Childhood is a unique and valuable stage in the life cycle. Our paramount responsibility is to provide safe, healthy, nurturing, and responsive settings for children. We are committed to support children's development, respect individual differences, help children learn to live and work cooperatively, and promote health, self-awareness, competence, self-worth, and resiliency.

Ideals

I-1.1. To be familiar with the knowledge base of early childhood care and education and to keep current through continuing education and in-service training.

I-1.2. To base program practices upon current knowledge in the field of child development and related disciplines and upon particular knowledge of each child.

I-1.3. To recognize and respect the uniqueness and the potential of each child.

I-1.4. To appreciate the special vulnerability of children.

I-1.5.   To create and maintain safe and healthy settings that foster children's social, emotional, intellectual, and physical development and that respect their dignity and their contributions.

I-1.6.   To support the right of each child to play and learn in inclusive early childhood programs to the fullest extent consistent with the best interests of all involved. As with adults who are disabled in the larger community, children with disabilities are ideally served in the same settings in which they would participate if they did not have a disability.

I-1.7.   To ensure that children with disabilities have access to appropriate and convenient support services and to advocate for the resources necessary to provide the most appropriate settings for all children.

Principles

P-1.1.   Above all, we shall not harm children. We shall not participate in practices that are disrespectful, degrading, dangerous, exploitative, intimidating, emotionally damaging, or physically harmful to children. This principle has precedence over all others in this Code.

P-1.2.   We shall not participate in practices that discriminate against children by denying benefits, giving special advantages, or excluding them from programs or activities on the basis of their race, ethnicity, religion, sex, national origin, language, ability, or the status, behavior, or beliefs of their parents. (This principle does not apply to programs that have a lawful mandate to provide services to a particular population of children.)

P-1.3.   We shall involve all of those with relevant knowledge (including staff and parents) in decisions concerning a child.

P-1.4.   For every child we shall implement adaptations in teaching strategies, learning environment, and curricula; consult with the family; and seek recommendations from appropriate specialists to maximize the potential of the child to benefit from the program. If, after these efforts have been made to work with a child and family, the child does not appear to be benefiting from a program, or the child is seriously jeopardizing the ability of other children to benefit from the program, we shall communicate with the family and appropriate specialists to determine the child's current needs; identify the setting and services most suited to meeting these needs; and assist the family in placing the child in an appropriate setting.

P-1.5.   We shall be familiar with the symptoms of child abuse, including physical, sexual, verbal, and emotional abuse, and neglect. We shall know and follow state laws and community procedures that protect children against abuse and neglect.

P-1.6.   When we have reasonable cause to suspect child abuse or neglect, we shall report it to the appropriate community agency and follow up to ensure that appropriate action has been taken. When appropriate, parents or guardians will be informed that the referral has been made.

P-1.7.   When another person tells us of a suspicion that a child is being abused or neglected, we shall assist that person in taking appropriate action to protect the child.

P-1.8.   When a child protective agency fails to provide adequate protection for abused or neglected children, we acknowledge a collective ethical responsibility to work toward improvement of these services.

P-1.9.   When we become aware of a practice or situation that endangers the health or safety of children, but has not been previously known to do so, we have an ethical responsibility to inform those who can remedy the situation and who can protect children from similar danger.

Section II: Ethical Responsibilities to Families

Families are of primary importance in children's development. (The term *family* may include others, besides parents, who are responsibly involved with the child.) Because the family and the early childhood practitioner have a common interest in the child's welfare, we acknowledge a primary responsibility to bring about collaboration between the home and school in ways that enhance the child's development.

Ideals

I-2.1.   To develop relationships of mutual trust with families we serve.

I-2.2.   To acknowledge and build upon strengths and competencies as we support families in their task of nurturing children.

I-2.3.   To respect the dignity of each family and its culture, language, customs, and beliefs.

I-2.4.   To respect families' child rearing values and their right to make decisions for their children.

I-2.5.   To interpret each child's progress to parents within the framework of a developmental perspective and to help families understand and appreciate the value of developmentally appropriate early childhood practices.

I-2.6.   To help family members improve their understanding of their children and to enhance their skills as parents.

I-2.7.   To participate in building support networks for families by providing them with opportunities to interact with program staff, other families, community resources, and professional services.

Principles

P-2.1.   We shall not deny family members access to their child's classroom or program setting.

P-2.2.   We shall inform families of program philosophy, policies, and personnel qualifications, and explain why we teach as we do, which should be in accordance with our ethical responsibilities to children (see Section I).

P-2.3.   We shall inform families of, and when appropriate, involve them in policy decisions.

P-2.4.   We shall involve families in significant decisions affecting their child.

P-2.5.   We shall inform the family of accidents involving their child, of risks such as exposures to contagious disease that may result in infection, and of occurrences that might result in emotional stress.

P-2.6. To improve the quality of early childhood care and education, we shall cooperate with qualified child development researchers. Families shall be fully informed of any proposed research projects involving their children and shall have the opportunity to give or withhold consent without penalty. We shall not permit or participate in research that could in any way hinder the education, development, or well-being of children.

P-2.7. We shall not engage in or support exploitation of families. We shall not use our relationship with a family for private advantage or personal gain, or enter into relationships with family members that might impair our effectiveness in working with children.

P-2.8. We shall develop written policies for the protection of confidentiality and the disclosure of children's records. These policy documents shall be made available to all program personnel and families. Disclosure of children's records beyond family members, program personnel, and consultants having an obligation of confidentiality shall require familial consent (except in cases of abuse or neglect).

P-2.9. We shall maintain confidentiality and shall respect the family's right to privacy, refraining from disclosure of confidential information and intrusion into family life. However, when we have reason to believe that a child's welfare is at risk, it is permissible to share confidential information with agencies and individuals who may be able to intervene in the child's interest.

P-2.10. In cases where family members are in conflict, we shall work openly, sharing our observations of the child, to help all parties involved make informed decisions. We shall refrain from becoming an advocate for one party.

P-2.11. We shall be familiar with and appropriately use community resources and professional services that support families. After a referral has been made, we shall follow up to ensure that services have been appropriately provided.

Section III. Ethical Responsibilities to Colleagues

In a caring, cooperative workplace, human dignity is respected, professional satisfaction is promoted, and positive relationships are modeled. Based upon our core values, our primary responsibility in this arena is to establish and maintain settings and relationships that support productive work and meet professional needs. The same ideals that apply to children are inherent in our responsibilities to adults.

A. Responsibilities to Co-Workers

Ideals

I-3A.1. To establish and maintain relationships of respect, trust, and cooperation with co-workers.

I-3A.2. To share resources and information with co-workers.

I-3A.3. To support co-workers in meeting their professional needs and in their professional development.

P-3A.4. To accord co-workers due recognition of professional achievement.

Principles

P-3A.1. When we have concern about the professional behavior of a co-worker, we shall first let that person know of our concern in a way that shows respect for personal dignity and for the diversity to be found among staff members, and then attempt to resolve the matter collegially.

P-3A.2. We shall exercise care in expressing views regarding the personal attributes or professional conduct of co-workers. Statements should be based on firsthand knowledge and relevant to the interests of children and programs.

B. Responsibilities to Employers

Ideals

I-3B.1. To assist the program in providing the highest quality of service.

I-3B.2. To do nothing that diminishes the reputation of the program in which we work unless it is violating laws and regulations designed to protect children or the provisions of this Code.

Principles

P-3B.1. When we do not agree with program policies, we shall first attempt to effect change through constructive action within the organization.

P-3B.2. We shall speak or act on behalf of an organization only when authorized. We shall take care to acknowledge when we are speaking for the organization and when we are expressing a personal judgment.

P-3B.3. We shall not violate laws or regulations designed to protect children and shall take appropriate action consistent with this Code when aware of such violations.

C. Responsibilities to Employees

Ideals

I-3C.1. To promote policies and working conditions that foster mutual respect, competence, well-being, and positive self-esteem in staff members.

I-3C.2. To create a climate of trust and candor that will enable staff to speak and act in the best interests of children, families, and the field of early childhood care and education.

I-3C.3. To strive to secure equitable compensation (salary and benefits) for those who work with or on behalf of young children.

Principles

P-3C.1. In decisions concerning children and programs, we shall appropriately utilize the education, training, experience, and expertise of staff members.

P-3C.2. We shall provide staff members with safe and supportive working conditions that permit them to carry out their responsibilities, timely and nonthreatening evaluation procedures, written grievance procedures, constructive feedback, and opportunities for continuing professional development and advancement.

P-3C.3. We shall develop and maintain comprehensive written personnel policies that define program standards and, when applicable, that specify the extent to which employees are accountable for their conduct outside the workplace. These policies shall be given to new staff members and shall be available for review by all staff members.

P-3C.4. Employees who do not meet program standards shall be informed of areas of concern and, when possible, assisted in improving their performance.

P-3C.5. Employees who are dismissed shall be informed of the reasons for their termination. When a dismissal is for cause, justification must be based on evidence of inadequate or inappropriate behavior that is accurately documented, current, and available for the employee to review.

P-3C.6. In making evaluations and recommendations, judgments shall be based on fact and relevant to the interests of children and programs.

P-3C.7. Hiring and promotion shall be based solely on a person's record of accomplishment and ability to carry out the responsibilities of the position.

P-3C.8. In hiring, promotion, and provision of training, we shall not participate in any form of discrimination based on race, ethnicity, religion, gender, national origin, culture, disability, age, or sexual preference. We shall be familiar with and observe laws and regulations that pertain to employment discrimination.

Section IV: Ethical Responsibilities to Community and Society

Early childhood programs operate within a context of an immediate community made up of families and other institutions concerned with children's welfare. Our responsibilities to the community are to provide programs that meet its needs, to cooperate with agencies and professions that share responsibility for children, and to develop needed programs that are not currently available. Because the larger society has a measure of responsibility for the welfare and protection of children, and because of our specialized expertise in child development, we acknowledge an obligation to serve as a voice for children everywhere.

Ideals

I-4.1. To provide the community with high-quality (age and individually appropriate and culturally and socially sensitive) education/care programs and services.

I-4.2. To promote cooperation among agencies and interdisciplinary collaboration among professions concerned with the welfare of young children, their families, and their teachers.

I-4.3. To work, through education, research, and advocacy, toward an environmentally safe world in which all children receive adequate health care, food, and shelter, are nurtured, and live free from violence.

I-4.4. To work, through education, research, and advocacy, toward a society in which all young children have access to high-quality education/care programs.

I-4.5. To promote knowledge and understanding of young children and their needs. To work toward greater social acknowledgment of children's rights and greater social acceptance of responsibility for their well-being.

I-4.6.   To support policies and laws that promote the well-being of children and families and to oppose those that impair their well-being. To participate in developing policies and laws that are needed and to cooperate with other individuals and groups in these efforts.

I-4.7.   To further the professional development of the field of early childhood care and education and to strengthen its commitment to realizing its core values as reflected in this Code.

Principles

P-4.1.   We shall communicate openly and truthfully about the nature and extent of services that we provide.

P-4.2.   We shall not accept or continue to work in positions for which we are personally unsuited or professionally unqualified. We shall not offer services that we do not have the competence, qualifications, or resources to provide.

P-4.3.   We shall be objective and accurate in reporting the knowledge upon which we base our program practices.

P-4.4.   We shall cooperate with other professionals who work with children and their families.

P-4.5.   We shall not hire or recommend for employment any person whose competence, qualifications, or character makes him or her unsuited for the position.

P-4.6.   We shall report the unethical or incompetent behavior of a colleague to a supervisor when informal resolution is not effective.

P-4.7.   We shall be familiar with laws and regulations that serve to protect the children in our programs.

P-4.8.   We shall not participate in practices which are in violation of laws and regulations that protect the children in our programs.

P-4.9.   When we have evidence that an early childhood program is violating laws or regulations protecting children, we shall report it to persons responsible for the program. If compliance is not accomplished within a reasonable time, we will report the violation to appropriate authorities who can be expected to remedy the situation.

P-4.10. When we have evidence that an agency or a professional charged with providing services to children, families, or teachers is failing to meet its obligations, we acknowledge a collective ethical responsibility to report the problem to appropriate authorities or to the public.

P-4.11. When a program violates or requires its employees to violate this Code, it is permissible, after fair assessment of the evidence, to disclose the identity of that program.

Statement of Commitment

As an individual who works with young children, I commit myself to furthering the values of early childhood education as they are reflected in the NAEYC Code of Ethical Conduct.

To the best of my ability I will:

◆ Ensure that programs for young children are based on current knowledge of child development and early childhood education.

- Respect and support families in their task of nurturing children.
- Respect colleagues in early childhood education and support them in maintaining the NAEYC Code of Ethical Conduct.
- Serve as an advocate for children, their families, and their teachers in community and society.
- Maintain high standards of professional conduct.
- Recognize how personal values, opinions, and biases can affect professional judgment.
- Be open to new ideas and be willing to learn from the suggestions of others.
- Continue to learn, grow, and contribute as a professional.
- Honor the ideals and principles of the NAEYC Code of Ethical Conduct.

This document is an official position statement of the National Association for the Education of Young Children.

APPENDIX I

Child Development Permit Matrix

Title	Educational requirement	Experience requirement	Alternative qualifications	Authorization	Five-year renewal
Assistant (optional)	6 units* of early childhood education (ECE) or child development (CD)	None	Accredited HERO program (including ROCP); or CCTC-approved training	Assist in the instruction of children under supervision of Associate Teacher or above	105 hours of professional growth
Associate Teacher	12 units of ECE/CD, including core courses†	50 days of 3 + hours per day within 2 years	Child Development Associate (CDA) Credential; or CCTC-approved training	May provide instruction and supervise Assistant	Must meet teacher requirements within 10 years
Teacher	24 units of ECE/CD, including core courses + 16 general education (GE) units‡	175 days of 3 + hours per day within 4 years	AA or higher in ECE or related field with 3 semester units of supervised field experience in ECE setting; or CCTC-approved training	May provide instruction and supervise all above (including Aide)	105 hours of professional growth
Master Teacher	24 units ECE/CD, including core courses + 16 GE units + 6 specialization units; + 2 adult supervision units	350 days of 3 + hours per day within 4 years	BA or higher with 12 units of ECE + 3 semester units of supervised field experience in ECE setting; or CCTC-approved training	May provide instruction and supervise all above (including Aide). May also serve as coordinator of curriculum and staff development	105 hours of professional growth
Site Supervisor	AA (or 60 units) with 24 ECE/CD units (including core); + 6 units administration; + 2 units adult supervision	350 days of 3 + hours per day within 4 years, including at least 100 days of supervising adults	BA or higher with 12 units of ECE + 3 units of supervised field experience in ECE setting; or a Teaching or an Administrative credential with 12 units of ECE, + 3 units supervised field experience in ECE setting, or CCTC-approved training	May supervise single-site program, provide instruction, and serve as coordinator of curriculum and staff development	105 hours of professional growth
Program Director	BA with 24 ECE/CD units (including core) + 6 units administration; + 2 units adult supervision	Site supervisor status and one program year of site supervisor experience	Teaching or Administrative credential with 12 units of ECE + 3 units of supervised field experience in an ECE setting; or CCTC-approved training; master's degree in ECE or CD	May supervise multiple-site program, provide instruction, and serve as coordinator of curriculum and staff development	105 hours of professional growth

*A *unit* is the California term used to refer to college credits. Thus, six units equals six college credits.
†Core courses are child growth and development; child/family/community; program/curriculum.
‡The general education requirement is one course in each of four general education categories: English, mathematics or science, social science, and the humanities.
HERO = Home Economics Related Occupations.
ROCP = Regional Occupational Center Program.
CCTC = California Commission on Teacher Credentialing.
Adopted by the California Commission on Teacher Credentialing, February 1, 1997.
From: Burton, A., and M. Whitebook. 1998. *Child Care Staff Compensation Guidelines for California, 1998.* Washington, D.C.: Center for the Child Care Workforce, p. 19.

This publication is one of over 700 that are available from the California Department of Education. Some of the more recent publications or those most widely used are the following:

Item no.	Title (Date of publication)	Price
1379	Assessing and Fostering the Development of a First and a Second Language in Early Childhood—Training Manual (1998)	$19.00
1377	Assessing the Development of a First and a Second Language in Early Childhood: Resource Guide (1998)	10.75
1436	California Department of Education Early Start Program Guide (1998)	10.00
1491	Collaborative Partners: California's Experience with the 1997 Head Start Expansion Grants (2000)	12.50
1285	Continuity for Young Children (1997)	7.50
1431	Early Identification/Early Intervention of Young Children with Emotional and Behavioral Issues: Trainer of Trainers Manual (1998)	30.00
1410	Ear-Resistible: Hearing Test Procedures for Infants, Toddlers, and Preschoolers, Birth Through Five Years of Age (1998)	10.00
1011	Exemplary Program Standards for Child Development Programs Serving Preschool and School-Age Children (1991)	8.00
1124	Exemplary Program Standards for Child Development Programs Serving Preschool and School-Age Children (Spanish) (1994)	8.00
1010	Exemplary Program Standards: How to Conduct Your Agency Self-Study (video) (1992)	15.95
1106	Exemplary Program Standards: How to Conduct Your Agency Self-Study (Spanish) (video) (1993)	15.95
1367	Family Connections: Helping Caregivers Develop Nutrition Partnerships with Parents (1997)	9.00
1475	First Class: A Guide for Early Primary Education, Preschool–Kindergarten–First Grade (1999)	15.00
1388	First Look: Vision Evaluation and Assessment for Infants, Toddlers, and Preschoolers, Birth Through Five Years of Age (1998)	10.00
1378	Fostering the Development of a First and a Second Language in Early Childhood: Resource Guide (1998)	10.75
1465	Handbook on Administration of Early Childhood Special Education Programs (2000)	13.50
0737	Here They Come: Ready or Not—Report of the School Readiness Task Force (summary report) (1988)	5.00
1252	Just Kids: A Training Manual for Working with Children Prenatally Substance-Exposed (1996)	22.25
1227	Keeping Kids Healthy: Preventing and Managing Communicable Disease in Child Care (1995)	15.00*
1152	Kids' Time: A School-Age Care Program Guide (1994)	11.50
1486	Kids' Time: A School-Age Care Program Guide (Spanish) (El Horario de los Niños) (2000)	14.95
1265	Kids' Time: Planning School-Age Care Activities (video and booklet) (1996)	17.00
1257	Kids' Time: Planning School-Age Care Activities (Spanish) (video and booklet) (1996)	17.00
1384	Observing Preschoolers: Assessing First and Second Language Development (video) (1998)	12.00
1256	Project EXCEPTIONAL: A Guide for Training and Recruiting Child Care Providers to Serve Young Children with Disabilities, Volume 1 (1996)	20.00
1257	Project EXCEPTIONAL: A Guide for Training and Recruiting Child Care Providers to Serve Young Children with Disabilities, Volume 2 (1996)	30.75
1399	Ready to Learn—Quality Preschools for California in the 21st Century: The Report of the Superintendent's Universal Preschool Task Force (1998)	8.00
1315	Reducing Exceptional Stress and Trauma: Curriculum and Intervention Guidelines (1997)	17.00
1316	Reducing Exceptional Stress and Trauma: Facilitator's Guide (1997)	18.00
1383	Talking with Preschoolers: Strategies for Promoting First and Second Language Development (video) (1998)	12.00
1255	Taking Charge: A Disaster Preparedness Guide for Child Care and Development Centers (1996)	10.25
1260	Today's Special: A Fresh Approach to Meals for Preschoolers (video and guide) (1996)	17.00†

*Companion videos are available in English (item no. 9842) and Spanish (item no. 1212) at $17.00 each.

†Also available in a Spanish edition of both video and guide (item no. 1262) at same price.

Orders should be directed to:

California Department of Education
CDE Press, Sales Office
P.O. Box 271
Sacramento, CA 95812-0271

Please include the item number and desired quantity for each title ordered. Shipping and handling charges are additional, and purchasers in California also add county sales tax.

Mail orders must be accompanied by a check, a purchase order, or a credit card number, including expiration date (VISA or MasterCard only). Purchase orders without checks are accepted from educational institutions, businesses, and governmental agencies. Telephone orders will be accepted toll-free (1-800-995-4099) for credit card purchases. *All sales are final.*

The *Educational Resources Catalog* contains illustrated, annotated listings of departmental publications, videos, and other instructional materials. Free copies of the catalog may be obtained by writing to the address given above or by calling (916) 445-1260. Visit the Web site <http:www.cde.ca.gov/cdepress/catalog.html>.

Prices and availability are subject to change without notice. Please call 1-800-995-4099 for current prices and shipping charges.